Selected Poetry
of
Jessica Powers

**Edited by Regina Siegfried, ASC and
Robert F. Morneau**

Sheed & Ward

Publication Acknowledgements

Many of the poems selected for this edition have been published previously in the following magazines:

America	*Harper's*
American Mercury	*Poetry: A Magazine of Verse*
The Bible Today	*Sign*
New Catholic World	*Spirit*
Commonweal	*Spiritual Life*
The Forge	*Today*
The Franciscan	

The Belknap Press of Harvard University Press has granted permission to quote from Letter 955 of the letters of Emily Dickinson.

Sheed & Ward™ is a service of National Catholic Reporter Publishing, Inc.

Library of Congress Catalog Card Number: 88-63849

ISBN: 1-55612-248-9

Published by: Sheed & Ward
115 E. Armour Blvd. P.O. Box 419492
Kansas City, MO 64141

To order, call: (800) 333-7373

Dedication

For the members of Sister Miriam's community, the Carmelites of the Carmel of the Mother of God, Pewaukee, Wisconsin: Sisters Bernadette Ranallo, Mary Bernadette Medelska (died April 6, 1989), Mary Agnes Kramer, Mary Joyce King, Mary Gertrude Borg, and Marie Cecilia Ok-Hee Kim.

Acknowledgements

Emily Dickinson wrote: "The Thank you in my heart obstructs the Thank you on my Lips" (Letter 955, 1 Dec., 1884). We too have words of gratitude in our hearts that we need to express.

People who have been particularly supportive, interested, and encouraging in a variety of ways are: Rev. Bernard McGarty of La Crosse, WI, Sister Miriam's cousin; Dolores Leckey, executive director of the Secretariat on the Laity and Family and Sister Miriam's biographer; and members of Ruma province of Adorers of the Blood of Christ. Sister Pauline Grady, ASC and Sister Paula Lynch, ASC were meticulous, precise, and enthusiastic as proofreaders.

Marquette University Archives is the repository for Sister Miriam's manuscripts and papers as well as Sister Regina's research. Marquette's archivists, especially Mr. Charles Elston, deserve our words of thanks for their professional expertise.

Finally, Sister Miriam's community, to whom we dedicate this book, was always gracious, warm, and hospitable during our visits to the Carmel. They continue to welcome us as friends.

Sister Miriam herself knew of the close relationship between gratitude and love when she wrote:

The Gift of Love

My thoughts of you are fair as precious stones
out of the memory's deep mysterious mines.
I cut and polish, hold the gems to light—
color of sea water, color of wines,
coaxed from the earth's sweetest fruits. I drop them
                          down

into my heart, into the lifted hands
of love whose lone concern is your renown.

Contents

I.
Vision
The Mercy of God

II.
Of God and Angels, and other Glorious Things
God and Divine Mercy

Spirit and Fire

Love

Heaven

Mary and the Saints

Angels

Beauty: Music and Light and Color

Liturgical Seasons

III.
The Human Journey: The Agony and the Ecstasy

Creaturehood: Our Poverty and Aloneness

Journey of the Soul

Decisions

IV.
Of Birds and Rainbows, and
All Assorted Things
Nature and Grace

Birds and Lessons for Life

Introduction: The Mission of the Poet

In his work, *The Nigger of the Narcissus,* Joseph Conrad captures well the mission of the artist:

> To arrest, for the space of a breath, the hands busy about the work of the earth, and compel men entranced by the sight of distant goals to glance for a moment at the surrounding vision of form and colour, of sunshine and shadows; to make them pause for a look, a sigh, for a smile—such is the aim, difficult and evanescent, and reserved only for a very few to achieve. But sometimes, by the deserving and the fortunate, even that task is accomplished. And when it is accomplished—behold!—all the truth of life is there: a moment of vision, a sigh, a smile—and the return to an eternal rest. (29)

Jessica Powers is an artist, painting in words the movements of the heart, the aspirations of the soul, the homelessness of a pilgrim people, the joys and sufferings of the mystic, the song and dance of those in love, the beauties of creation. The reader of her verse will pause for a deep look into the solitude of God's presence, will be drawn, through wonder and awe, to sigh before the voluminous garments of God's mercy (see "The Garments of God"), will smile at the poet's claim that inebriation occurs in

the name of courtesy to a God who offers too much potent good-
ness.

But Not With Wine

O God of too much giving, whence is this
inebriation that possesses me,
that the staid road now wanders all amiss,
and that the wind walks much too giddily,
clutching a bush for balance, or a tree?
How then can dignity and pride endure
with such inordinate mirth upon the land,
when steps and speech are somewhat insecure
and the light heart is wholly out of hand?

If there be indecorum in my songs,
fasten the blame where rightly it belongs:
on Him who offered me too many cups
of His most potent goodness—not on me,
a peasant who, because a King was host,
drank out of courtesy.

* * * * *

Jessica Powers has written over four hundred poems, nearly
three hundred of which have been published in a variety of peri-
odicals including *America, Commonweal, Sign,* and many
others. She lived in the Carmel in Pewaukee, Wisconsin. Her
Scotch-Irish ancestry, her many years of rural living, her love of
St. John of the Cross, her desire to draw people into the
presence of God have all radically influenced her poetry and her
life.

Jessica Powers' ability to arrest our attention, we who live in
a frenzied century of activism and consumerism, is no small
achievement. Yet that ability is grounded in the fact that she is
able to be moved deeply by the words of others. Her poem,
"Come, South Wind," flows from St. John of the Cross where he

says, "By south wind is meant the Holy Spirit who awakens love." While a scripture scholar's comment that virtue puts the house at rest triggered the poem "The House at Rest," the poem also patently bears the mark of St. John of the Cross, and, less obviously, reflects the wisdom of St. Teresa of Jesus' dictum that, unless we practice the little virtues, we will remain spiritual dwarves. Her poem "The Leftovers" grew out of a homily that touched her heart. Grounded in the present moment, this poet is able to catch the stirrings of the Spirit because she is a listener and a lover.

William Carlos Williams, quoted in *Inner Companions,* specifies another dimension of the poet's mission:

> I wanted, if I was to write in a larger way than of birds and flowers, to write about the people close about me: to know in detail, minutely what I was talking about to the whites of their eyes, to their very smell. This is the poet's business. Not to talk in vague categories but to write particularly, as a physician works upon a patient, upon the things before him, in the particular to discover the universal... (78-79)

Poetry comes in a variety of forms. Emily Dickinson focuses some six hundred poems on the mystery of death and dying; Robert Frost leads us down the various paths of nature in delightful and rewarding ways, regardless of the roads we have not taken; Shakespeare's sonnets attempt to unravel the mysteries of love and human foibles. Jessica Powers' primary focus is on the *particular* grace, grace that is often submerged in suffering and great pain. Hers is primarily an interior topography of a God of a "thousand acres." Hers is a "trackless solitude" that each person must one day encounter. She startles us with the naked question: "Child, have none told you? *God* is in your soul."

While grounding us in the necessity of the poetic particular, the poems in this volume eventually draw us into the universal Love we call God. In the poem "Abraham" we encounter "that old weather-beaten nomad," watch how "his faith erupted him into a way far-off and strange," and ponder the question of how "his ancient thighs would bear nations." All these particulars, far from causing us to lose the essence of the question, flesh out the large universal question of our own "far and lonely journey, too." Because we come up close to other pilgrims on the journey, we understand a little better our own search.

Born in Mauston, Wisconsin, in 1905, Jessica Powers journeyed from this rural Wisconsin community to Marquette University (1922-1923) to secretarial work in Chicago. During those early years we find a young poet testing her wings and struggling to take flight. At times her poetry reflects longing and fulfillment, as in her first published poem in *American Poetry Magazine* (March-April, 1924): "Dreams of You." At other times it reveals a certain romanticism, as in "Had I Lived Long Ago" with its dreams of a pirate chief, ships and strange shores. Still, even in some of these early poems, one can see hints of future excellence in their crafty phrases and bold concreteness.

Dreams of You

My dreams of you are like the fallen leaves,
colored with brillance, nomad rustling things,
tossed by the winds of olden memories—
they prate of golden summertimes and springs.

When skies were gray you flung them all away—
but I, who loved them, hoard such gifts as these.
By day I revel in their gilded lights;
at night they whisper tender sympathies.

The poem "Had I Lived Long Ago," while demonstrating the romanticism of some early poems, also shows the adventuresome spirit that embarked Sister Miriam upon the solitary journey of her soul's search. The same spirit that would, in metaphoric language, "have wed a pirate chief" has close affinity with the spirit that eschews comfort, surety and ambition to risk the rugged road of Carmel.

Had I Lived Long Ago

I would have wed a pirate chief,
had I lived long and long ago,
and made my home a ship that rides
wherever winds can blow!

I would have made me daring songs
to fling against the sweeping gale—
gay songs of strange and plundered shores,
with notes like silver hail!

But years have made their jest of me.
Now I can only walk and sing
a song about a broken heart. . .
or any foolish thing.

* * * * *

In 1923, the fledgling poet returned to the farm for some ten years, after which she spent four years in New York where, in a time of general unemployment, she took care of children, living with Anton Pegis, the Thomistic philosopher, and his wife, Jessica. Her association with the Pegis children and their innocent life-views helped move her forward in her own search for wisdom. Moreover, such work freed her mind to concentrate on the deeper realities of life without the distraction of business concerns.

During these fertile, formative years in New York, she enjoyed opportunities for the friendly exchanges of an intellectual circle (she was a member of the Catholic Poetry Society of America) and a living environment of close and dear friends. By

1939 Jessica Powers manifested developed skills and deep insight. In contrast to her earlier poems we find a maturing poet. The poem "Human Winter" was written in 1940, a year before she entered the Carmelite monastery. Here we see the longing for that intense love which only God can give. The fire of faith alone can warm the depth of the soul.

Human Winter

No fire could warm this place
though the air hang in sultry shred and the roof
    perspire,
nothing here is amenable to fire.

Words fall in slow icy rain and freeze
upon the heart's sudden dismantled trees,
and branches break and fall.
From the wind of inclement glances I cannot shield
    myself
who find their frost too subtle to forestall.
I am waiting for the snow of my own obscurity to settle
and cover me, frozen ground,
to blunt all sharp insufferable sound,
to meet the angles of cold and obliterate them all.

I long to rise in this room and say, "You are not my
    people,
I come from a warm country, my country of love.
Nor did I wish to come here; I was misdirected."
But their frost is not defied and their cold is not
    rejected.
So chilled am I by this presence of human winter
I cannot speak or move.

* * * * *

In December of 1941 Jessica Powers entered the Carmelite community and made even vaster journeys into silence and solitude, following the tradition of John of the Cross and Teresa of Avila. She responded to the universal call to holiness in a particular way: religious life. From that particular situation Jessica Powers would articulate universal insights and questions offered to her in grace.

The poetic mission has something to do with "the refinement of the heart." Anthony Padovano, in his biography on Thomas Merton, *The Human Journey*, writes:

> For Merton, poetry had something to do with the refinement of the human heart. As his poetry developed, it became religious not in its content but in its capacity to deal with the spirit and to encounter the human. As we see in *Bread in the Wilderness*, poetry was for him a reality that "could not be produced by any other combination of words," a work of art that lived a life all its own. The point of the poem was not only aesthetic enchantment but contemplation and dialogue. Poetic experience, like religious experience, is an act of communion with the world. A poem is religious not because its intent is religious but because it intends contact with human experience on the deepest level possible. (81)

What is so attractive about the poetry of Jessica Powers is both its realism regarding the human condition and its affirmation of God and life. In an article entitled "Jessica Powers: The Paradox of Light and Dark," Sr. Regina Siegfried, ASC, writes: "Always aware of the dark side of human nature and of pain and purification as necessary companions on the journey, Jessica Powers nevertheless believes in light and chooses it. She is a contemporary poet in the ancient tradition of John of the Cross" (34).

The heart is refined by contact with reality at every level. Poetry that is grounded in contemplation and dialogue gives us access to the realities of the human heart: the reality of our authentic self, the reality of our basic homelessness and emptiness, the reality of God's mercy and abundant love. Away from reality, the heart withers. Disconnected from its source of love, the heart experiences anguish. The poetry of Jessica Powers leads to communion because its wellsprings flow out of human experience that is essentially expressive of the Incarnation. Sentimentality is seldom found in these verses because of deep faith and the beautiful rawness of our human poverty. Eudora Welty's "I had come unprepared for the immediacy of poetry" was and continues to remain my experience as I read and reread Jessica Powers' poems.

But who refines the poet's heart? For Jessica Powers there were many major influences that shaped her life and poetic vision: her family and the Carmelite community, her dear friends Jessica and Anton Pegis, her staunch supporter and first publisher, Clifford Laube, and her eighth-grade teacher, Sr. Lucille Massart, OP, who encouraged Jessica to write. Then there were the poets and mystics, first of all, St. John of the Cross. In an interview Sister Miriam tells how, when his books were recommended to her, "I bought them and carried them home as if I'd just purchased heaven!" She read Hopkins and Herbert and Emily Dickinson and the earlier writers. Later she encountered and appreciated the modern poets and found many poems of excellence in contemporary writing as she continued to feed her muse with new inspiration. But most of all the great Refiner was the Holy Spirit, a Spirit that tries the soul beyond belief and leads it out of the false self into the place of great splendor.

Between the lines of all her verse lies hidden the doctrine of the divine indwelling. We sensed, in interviews with Jessica Powers, that this was her mission: to draw people through the words into the presence of the Word. Only then can the heart be truly refined.

In a letter I received from Jessica Powers, written on Palm Sunday, 1987, she states: "My poetry department hasn't been tended to in years and is in disorder; I haven't found time to straighten it out, nor the ambition right now. My only purpose in writing is that these are things I would like to say to everyone, especially those who are turning from God. But I do not know if they would find grace in any words of mine." For others I cannot speak, but for myself I can. The poems of Jessica Powers are laden with grace. Anyone who enters into them with openness and faith will discover new splendors in creation and the burning lantern that abides in one's own soul.

Someone else can also speak about Jessica Powers. She is Sister Regina Siegfried, ASC, a religious from St. Louis, who has been following the writings of Jessica Powers since 1960. Since that time Sr. Regina has gathered together all the published and unpublished poetry of Jessica Powers. On a number of visits to the Carmel monastery, Sr. Regina has pursued the spirit behind this poetry and has described some of her observations in the article cited at the end of this introduction. Jessica Powers was grateful to Sr. Regina for her support and scholarly research.

During the past several years, Sr. Regina Siegfried and I worked with Jessica Powers to put together this selected edition of her poems. The project strengthened our friendship with Jessica Powers and deepened our admiration of her as a poet and a person. As a poet, Jessica is to be commended for her incisive clarity, powerful use of imagery, depth of perception and fidelity to the human condition. As a person, Jessica shared the gifts of humor, humility and gracious hospitality. Her love for God and for people who are afflicted was intense. Gracious is her poetic work because the poet was graced.

On July 9, 1988, Jessica Powers met with us to complete and approve the final version of the manuscript. That she was pleased, happy and peaceful about the manuscript has made our work all the more gratifying. This is indeed her book; it is our privilege to have been the editors.

After suffering a stroke on August 17, Jessica Powers died on August 18, 1988 at the age of 83. The last stanza of "The Ledge of Light" is a fitting statement about her own life and death:

Ah, but when love grows unitive I know
joy will upsoar, my heart sing, far more free,
having come home to God's infinity.

Another of her poems, "The Homecoming" served as a memorial card for the wake and funeral:

The spirit, newly freed from earth,
is all amazed at the surprise
of her belonging: suddenly
as native to eternity
to see herself, to realize
the heritage that lets her be
at home where all this glory lies.

By naught foretold could she have guessed
such welcome home: the robe, the ring,
music and endless banqueting,
these people hers, this place of rest
known, as of long remembering,
herself a child of God and pressed
with warm endearments to His breast.

One of my favorite poems is "The Garments of God." I share it both as an introduction to this collection as well as a basic summary of Jessica Powers' poetic theology. She said to a friend in prose: "All that we have is the mercy of God." She says to us in verse:

The Garments of God

God sits on a chair of darkness in my soul.
He is God alone, supreme in His majesty.

I sit at His feet, a child in the dark beside Him;
my joy is aware of His glance and my sorrow is
    tempted
to nest on the thought that His face is turned from me.
He is clothed in the robes of His mercy, voluminous
    garments—
not velvet or silk and affable to the touch,
but fabric strong for a frantic hand to clutch,
and I hold to it fast with the fingers of my will.
Here is my cry of faith, my deep avowal
to the Divinity that I am dust.
Here is the loud profession of my trust.
I need not go abroad
to the hills of speech and hinterlands of music
for a crier to walk in my soul where all is still.
I have this potent prayer through good or ill:
here in the dark I clutch the garments of God.

—Introduction by Robert Morneau,
    Auxiliary Bishop of Green Bay, Wisconsin

Works Cited

Conrad, Joseph. *The Nigger of the Narcissus*. (New York: Dell Publishing Company, Inc., 1963).

McCarthy, Colman. *Inner Companions*. (Washington, D.C.: Acropolis Books Ltd., 1975). Quotation from William Carlos Williams.

Padovano, Anthony T. *The Human Journey—Thomas Merton: Symbol of a Century*. (New York: Doubleday & Company, Inc., 1982).

Siegfried, Regina, ASC. "Jessica Powers: The Paradox of Light and Dark." *Studia Mystica*, 7, No. 1 (Spring, 1984): 28-45.

Notes

The dates at the end of the poems indicate the year(s) when the poem was published. If two dates appear, that means that the poem was published twice in different magazines or books.

The ordering of the poems was done in this fashion. The ten introductory poems present a vision of Jessica Powers' world. Then three major divisions are made: poems dealing with the mystery of God and various attributes of divine life; poems dealing with the human condition and the use of freedom; poems dealing with nature and the seasons. The collection ends with the poem "Doxology," a poem of praise to a loving and merciful triune God. Jessica Powers concluded *The Place of Splendor* and *The House at Rest* with "Doxology"; it was her wish that this edition also end with the same poem.

Selected Poetry

of

Jessica Powers

Jessica Powers at work in January, 1988,
about seven months before she died.

I. Vision
The Mercy of God

The Mercy of God

I am copying down in a book from my heart's archives
the day that I ceased to fear God with a shadowy fear.
Would you name it the day that I measured my column of
virtue
and sighted through windows of merit a crown that was
near?
Ah, no, it was rather the day I began to see truly
that I came forth from nothing and ever toward nothing-
ness tend,
that the works of my hands are a foolishness wrought in
the presence
of the worthiest king in a kingdom that never shall end.
I rose up from the acres of self that I tended with passion
and defended with flurries of pride;
I walked out of myself and went into the woods of God's
mercy,
and here I abide.
There is greenness and calmness and coolness, a soft leafy
covering
from the judgment of sun overhead,
and the hush of His peace, and the moss of His mercy to
tread.
I have naught but my will seeking God; even love burning
in me
is a fragment of infinite loving and never my own.
And I fear God no more; I go forward to wander forever
in a wilderness made of His infinite mercy alone.

(1948)

1

The Vision

He said: write down the vision that you had,
and I wrote what I saw.

I saw the world kissing its own darkness.

It happened thus: I rose to meet the sunrise
and suddenly over the hill a horde appeared
dragging a huge tarpaulin.
They covered unwary land and hapless city
and all sweet water and fields.
And there was no sunrise.

I strained my eyes for a path and there was no path.
I bumped into trees and the bushes hissed at me,
and the long-armed brambles cried in a strident voice:
never through here!
But I struggled on, fumbling my beads of no.

I came to a dark city were nobody knew
that there was darkness.
And strange! though there was no light I still could see
what I did not want to see:
people who moved to the loveless embrace of folly.
They ate her gourmet foods; they drank her wine,
danced to her music that was crazed with rhythm,
were themselves discord though they knew it not,
or if they knew, cared less.

Outside the city wall I stood in thought,
parried a moment with a frightening urge
to court the darkness;
but I held back, fearing the face of love.

Crossing a field I wandered through a desert
when suddenly behind a rock I found
a little sagebrush where a fire was burning,
shining and dancing. After my first amazed
worship of silence I was loud with praise.

I watched with fear the darkness circling it,
lunging against it, swirling a black cloak
to suffocate the light,
until the shades broke loose and one by one
in terror fled.

The flame burned on, innocent, unimperiled.
There was no darkness that could put it out.

(revised for THaR, 1984)

The Legend of the Sparrow

(For a child who dreams of sainthood)

There was a sparrow once who dreamed to fly
into the sun.
Oh, how the birds of earth set up a cry
at such imprudence in a little one
when even eagles dared not venture near
the burning stratosphere.

"She will come down within a mile or two,"
they prophesied with dread.
It was, of course, most pitifully true.
Scarce half-way up the mountain overhead
she crashed into her feathers, as they said.

But when her wings healed, up she shot again
and sought a further bough.
She was more humble and more cautious now,
after a brief novitiate of pain.

Three times she rose; twice the wind brought her down,
once her own weariness.
At last she clutched a branch in her distress
and cried, "How can I ever hope to rest
in the sun's downy nest?
I faint; I fall whatever way I go!"

But then she turned and saw the home she left
unnumbered miles below,
while just beyond her lay the mountain top,
a kerchiefed head of snow.

Nobody told her and she never guessed
that earth's last height was all that she need seek.
All winds blow upward from the mountain peak
and there the sun has such magnetic rays

that in one moment she was lifted up
into his tender blaze.

Down in the valley there was such a stir:
A sparrow reached the sun!
Why had the wind and weather favored her?
What had she ever done?
Yet since they must, they spoke the praising word,
measured her flight and paused to gasp afresh.
What was she really but a little bird,
all feather and no flesh?

Only the sun knew, and the moving air
the miracle thereof:
a bird that wings itself with resolute love
can travel anywhere.

(1946)

This Trackless Solitude

Deep in the soul the acres lie
of virgin lands, of sacred wood
where waits the Spirit. Each soul bears
this trackless solitude.

The Voice invites, implores in vain
the fearful and the unaware;
but she who heeds and enters in
finds ultimate wisdom there.

The Spirit lights the way for her;
bramble and brush are pushed apart.
He lures her into wilderness
but to rejoice her heart.

Beneath the glistening foliage
the fruit of love hangs always near,
the one immortal fruit: *He is*
or, tasted: *He is here.*

Love leads and she surrenders to
His will, His waylessness of grace.
She speaks no word save His, nor moves
until He marks the place.

Hence all her paths are mystery,
presaging a divine unknown.
Her only light is in the creed
that she is not alone.

The soul that wanders, Spirit led,
becomes, in His transforming shade,
the secret that she was, in God,
before the world was made.

(1984)

And Wilderness Rejoices

Land that was desolate, impassable,
is forest now where secrets find their voices.
The desert is inhabited and blooms.
One with the meadow, wilderness rejoices.

Lebanon's glory is its green possession
and Carmel's beauty. Visited by love,
wastelands are pastures for the Lamb at midday,
And living solitudes to hold the Dove.

Never again will patriarch prefigure
or lean precursor walk or prophet call.
Here is fulfillment. One has come and given
the Spirit Who is flame and festival.

Sower and Sown are here. The bright groves flourish
and burn toward islands in the utmost sea.
Time has become a wilderness of presence
which too is essence of its jubilee.

Earth keeps its seasons and its liturgy,
as should the soul. Oh, come, green summer, blur
these wastes and let my soul in song declare
Who came by flesh and Who by fire to her.

(1952; 1984)

The Mountains of the Lord

Innocence never lost and innocence restored—
these two went up the mountains of the Lord.
And I addressed them, glowing and intense:
under the auspices of innocence
what amid holy places did you see?
And the untarnished spirit answered me:

> I saw a City gleaming on a hill,
> and one triumphant road divined its site.
> I saw a Fire no storm could ever still,
> feeding upon the branches of delight.
>
> I heard a Harp pluck its own serenade;
> I drank the Living Water from cool streams.
> I breathed the Wind that blows far down earth's shade
> The scent of petals from eternal dreams.
>
> Tables were spread on greensward and in grove
> with Bread the angels coveted afar.
> I walked beneath the shadow of a Dove
> who made a marriage with a Morningstar.
>
> Then I went upward where the summits glistened,
> lighted by love, the unconsuming flame.
> I heard a Voice, and when I stopped and listened
> it was the Bridegroom's voice and called my name.

I questioned innocence renewed by grace:
what did you see on hills beatified?
What voices heard you in the holy place?
With words of light the penitent replied:

> Under the night's impenetrable cover
> wherein I walked beset by many fears,
> I saw the radiant face of Christ the Lover,
> and it was wet with tears.

(1938; 1939)

8

Morning of Fog

Between this city of death with its gray face
and the city of life where my thoughts stir wild and free
a day stands. It is a road I trace
too eagerly.

For morning can give me nothing but a dull
cold sense of having died. The towers lift
like dreams. Down through the streets the beautiful
gray fogs of sorrow drift.

This is a city of phantoms. I am lost
in a place where nothing that beats with life should
roam.
Only a spirit chilled into a ghost
could call these streets its home.

I shall go exiled to the fall of night,
until I can return
to the city I love where the streets are washed with light
and the windows burn.

(1939)

The Uninvited

There is a city that through time shall lie
in a fixed darkness of the earth and sky;
and many dwell therein this very hour.
It is a city without seed or flower,
estranged from every bird and butterfly.

Who walked these streets of night? I know them well.
Those who come out of life's sequestered places:
the lonely, the unloved, the weak and shy,
the broken-winged who piteously would fly,
the poor who still have starlight in their faces.

They are the outcast ones, the last, the least,
whom earth has not invited to her feast,
and who, were they invited in the end,
finding their wedding clothes too frayed to mend,
would not attend.

(1935; 1939)

The Mystical Sparrow of St. John of the Cross

"Lost in the fathomless abyss of God."
                    —*The Spiritual Canticle*

Distantly pure and high, a mountain sparrow
is solitary in transfigured sky.
A ball of bird melodious with God
is lightsome in its love.
Not to dear mate or comrade do I cry
but to my own remote identity
who knows my spirit as divinely summoned
to gain that perch where no horizons lie.

Here is the king's secret scattered when I focus
unworthy song on one small eremite
lost in infinities of airy desert
where love is breathed out of the breast of light.

For call, for meeting-place, good end and rest
each has a symbol; each invokes a sign.
I take a bird in vastness and on height
to mark my love. It sings its jubilation
alone upon the housetop of creation
where earth's last finger touches the divine.

                    (1972)

II.
Of God and Angels, and other Glorious Things

God and Divine Mercy

God Is Today

God is today.
He is not yesterday.
He is not tomorrow.

God is the dawn, wakening earth to life;
the first morning ever,
shining with infinite innocence; a revelation
older than all beginning, younger than youth.
God is the noon, blinding the eye of the mind
with the blaze of truth.
God is the sunset, casting over creation
a color of glory
as He withdraws into mysteries of light.

God is today.
He is not yesterday.
He is not tomorrow.
He never is night.

Repairer of Fences

I am alone in the dark, and I am thinking
what darkness would be mine if I could see
the ruin I wrought in every place I wandered
and if I could not be
aware of One who follows after me.
Whom do I love, O God, when I love Thee?
The great Undoer who has torn apart
the walls I built against a human heart,
the Mender who has sewn together the hedges
through which I broke when I went seeking ill,
the Love who follows and forgives me still.
Fumbler and fool that I am, with things around me
of fragile make like souls, how I am blessed
to hear behind me footsteps of a Savior!
I sing to the east; I sing to the west:
God is my repairer of fences, turning my paths into rest.

Isaiah 58:12 (Douay)
(1952; 1984)

The Mystic Face

I never try to probe the sky's blue span;
I never look too deep into the sea
But the dim face of a tragedian
looks out at me.

Neither the night nor day can find a place
where I have not been shaken with surprise
at the white beauty of a holy face
and two great lonely eyes.

(1930; 1939)

God Is a Strange Lover

God is the strangest of all lovers; His ways are past explaining.
He sets His heart on a soul; He says to Himself, "Here will
                                        I rest My love."
But He does not woo her with flowers or jewels or words that
                                        are set to music,
no names endearing, no kindled praise His heart's direction
                                        prove.
His jealousy is an infinite thing. He stalks the soul
                                        with sorrows;
He tramples the bloom; He blots the sun that could make
                                        her vision dim.
He robs and breaks and destroys—there is nothing at last but
                                        her own shame, her own affliction,
and then He comes and there is nothing in the vast world but
                                        Him and her love of Him.

Not till the great rebellions die and her will is safe in His
                                        hands forever
does He open the door of light and His tendernesses fall,
and then for what is seen in the soul's virgin places,
for what is heard in the heart, there is no speech at all.

God is a strange lover; the story of His love is most surprising.
There is no proud queen in her cloth of gold; over and over again
there is only, deep in the soul, a poor disheveled woman
    weeping . . .
for us who have need of a picture and words: the Magdalen.

(1947; 1984)

16

But Not With Wine

"You are drunk, but not with wine."
                              Isaiah 51: 21.

O God of too much giving, whence is this
inebriation that possesses me,
that the staid road now wanders all amiss
and that the wind walks much too giddily,
clutching a bush for balance, or a tree?
How then can dignity and pride endure
with such inordinate mirth upon the land,
when steps and speech are somewhat insecure
and the light heart is wholly out of hand?

If there be indecorum in my songs,
fasten the blame where rightly it belongs:
on Him who offered me too many cups
of His most potent goodness—not on me,
a peasant who, because a king was host,
drank out of courtesy.

                              (1951; 1984)

Not Garden Any More

God is not garden any more, to satiate the senses
with the luxuriance of full exotic wilderness.
Now multiple is magnified to less.
God has become as desert now, a vast unknown Sahara
voicing its desert cry.
My soul has been arrested by the sound
of a divine tremendous loneliness.

I write anathema on pool, on streams of racing water.
I bid the shoot, the leaf, the bloom no longer to intrude.
Beyond green growth I find this greater good,
a motionless immensity of oneness.
And Him I praise Who lured me to this edge
of uncreation where His secrets brood,
Who seared the earth that I might hear in silence
this infinite outcry of His solitude.

(1950)

The Will of God

Time has one song alone. If you are heedful
and concentrate on sound with all your soul,
you may hear the song of the beautiful will of God,
soft notes or deep sonorous tones that roll
like thunder over time.
Not many have the hearing for this music,
and fewer still have sought it as sublime.

Listen, and tell your grief: But God is singing!
God sings through all creation with His will.
Save the negation of sin, all is His music,
even the notes that set their roots in ill
to flower in pity, pardon or sweet humbling.
Evil finds harshness of the rack and rod .
in tunes where good finds tenderness and glory.

The saints who loved have died of this pure music,
and no one enters heaven till he learns,
deep in his soul at least, to sing with God.

(1951)

The Kingdom of God

Not towards the stars, O beautiful naked runner,
not on the hills of the moon after a wild white deer,
seek not to discover afar the unspeakable wisdom,—
the quarry is here.

Beauty holds court within,—
a slim young virgin in a dim shadowy place.
Music is only the echo of her voice,
and earth is only a mirror for her face.

Not in the quiet arms, O sorrowful lover;
O fugitive, not in the dark on a pillow of breast;
hunt not under the lighted leaves for God,—
here is the sacred Guest.

There is a Tenant here.
Come home, roamer of earth, to this room and find
a timeless Heart under your own heart beating,
a Bird of beauty singing under your mind.

(1939)

The Garments of God

God sits on a chair of darkness in my soul.
He is God alone, supreme in His majesty.
I sit at His feet, a child in the dark beside Him;
my joy is aware of His glance and my sorrow is tempted
to nest on the thought that His face is turned from me.
He is clothed in the robes of His mercy, voluminous
   garments—
not velvet or silk and affable to the touch,
but fabric strong for a frantic hand to clutch,
and I hold to it fast with the fingers of my will.
Here is my cry of faith, my deep avowal
to the Divinity that I am dust.
Here is the loud profession of my trust.
I need not go abroad
to the hills of speech or the hinterlands of music
for a crier to walk in my soul where all is still.
I have this potent prayer through good or ill:
here in the dark I clutch the garments of God.

(1945; 1984)

The Ledge of Light

I have climbed up out of a narrow darkness
on to a ledge of light.
I am of God; I was not made for night.

Here there is room to lift my arms and sing.
Oh, God is vast! With Him all space can come
to hole or corner or *cubiculum*.

Though once I prayed, "O closed Hand holding me . . ."
I know Love, not a vise. I see aright,
set free in morning on this ledge of light.

Yet not all truth I see. Since I am not
yet one of God's partakers,
I visualize Him now: a thousand acres.

God is a thousand acres to me now
of high sweet-smelling April and the flow
of windy light across a wide plateau.

Ah, but when love grows unitive I know
joy will upsoar, my heart sing, far more free,
having come home to God's infinity.

(1967; 1984)

The Master Beggar

Worse than the poorest mendicant alive,
the pencil man, the blind man with his breath
of music shaming all who do not give,
are You to me, Jesus of Nazareth.

Must You take up Your post on every block
of every street? Do I have no release?
Is there no room of earth that I can lock
to Your sad face, Your pitiful whisper "Please"?

I seek the counters of time's gleaming store
but make no purchases, for You are there.
How can I waste one coin while you implore
with tear-soiled cheeks and dark blood-matted hair?

And when I offer You in charity
pennies minted by love, still, still You stand
fixing Your sorrowful wide eyes on me.
Must all my purse be emptied in Your hand?

Jesus, my beggar, what would You have of me?
Father and mother? the lover I longed to know?
The child I would have cherished tenderly?
Even the blood that through my heart's valves flow?

I too would be a beggar. Long tormented,
I dream to grant You all and stand apart
with You on some bleak corner, tear-frequented,
and trouble mankind for its human heart.

(1937)

23

The Cloister

Nobody lives in this shining house but God,
though shadowy figures tremble to and fro.
Over these cool grey stones that suffering made
only the pierced feet of the Master go.
A fire went through this place and gutted it;
over the ruins a fog of silence spread.
Nobody comes here but the pale young Christ
Who loves a shelter uninhabited.

Spirit and Fire

The First Pentecost

All the Apostles looked at one another;
words curled in fire through the returning gloom.
Something had changed and colored all the room.
The beauty of the Galilean mother
took the breath from them for a little space.
Even a cup, a chair or a brown dress
could draw their tears with the great loveliness
that wrote tremendous secrets every place.

That was the day when Fire came down from heaven,
inaugurating the first spring of love.
Blood melted in the frozen veins, and even
the least bird sang in the mind's inmost grove.
The seed sprang into flower, and over all
still do the multitudinous blossoms fall.

(1937)

The Wind of Pentecost

The Spirit lifts His inner crying,
and wind that on a ruined plain
sets a debris of echoes flying
does not so vehemently strain.

Whither, I ask, this rush of yearning
divinity? And dare I guess
that Love, the gale of God, is turning
towards acres of my nothingness?

Zephyr and gentle breeze they say You
and so You are in Your domain,
But if it please You, God, I pray You
possess me as a hurricane.

And name this as my consolation
who must be humbled since I sinned,
that death and loss and devastation
present no obstacle to wind.

O Love, vast and unabated,
make me Your wasteland, lone and lost,
divested earth alone created
to hold the Wind of Pentecost.

(1946)

This Is a Beautiful Time

This is a beautiful time, this last age, the age of
the Holy Spirit.
This is the long-awaited day of His reign in our
souls through grace.
He is crying to every soul that is walled:
Open to Me, My spouse, My sister.
And once inside, He is calling again:
Come to Me here in this secret place.
Oh, hear Him tonight crying all over the world
a last desperate summons of love to a dying race.

Acres we are to be gathered for God: He would pour
out His measureless morning
upon divinized lands, bought by blood, to their
Purchaser given.
Oh, hear Him within you speaking this infinite love,
moving like some divine and audible leaven,
lifting the sky of the soul with expansions of light,
shaping new heights and new depths,
and, at your stir of assent,
spreading the mountains with flame, filling the
hollows with heaven.

(1946; 1984)

Let There Be Light

Over the water of the world again
the Spirit broods;
Over the chaos the minds of all
and down the dream-deserted solitudes.

I know His ominous presence, and I hear
His prophecy of flight
over a world of thought at the first clear
and thunderous dismissal of the night.

How shall that burst of radiance be greeted
as, from the black abyss,
the first day wakens when it hears repeated
that cry to light, torn out of Genesis?

(1939)

O Spirita Sancta

O Spirita Sancta
soul to the Spirit wed,
dwell not upon Mount Sion
uncomforted.

Know that One dwells there
with you.
His breath is on your face,
though He wills not to ruffle
your bridal lace.

And yet your tears so
blind you
to your own sightliness
that you have not discovered
your wedding dress.

Nor do you know your dwelling
for dark is your retreat,
and who would guess that
darkness
could hold the Paraclete?

Since you are yet unworthy
His light is your distress,
the import of His nearness
your loneliness.

And yet He has been waiting,
the weary ages through,
until the hush of heaven
has entered you.

The Father seeks submission;
suffering draws the Son;
the Spirit though is only
by silence won.

Measure your love by
stillness.
He waits; do you as well
give to His infinite patience
your finite parallel.

God Himself is a silence,
seeking a soundless will.
O Spirita Sancta,
be very still.

When quiet has possessed you,
and dark has fled with dim,
you, on a mount of morning,
will be aware of Him.

(1945; 1984)

Shining Quarry

Since the luminous great wings of wonder stirred
over me in the twilight I have known
the Holy Spirit is the Poet's Bird.

Since in a wilderness I wandered near
a shining stag, this wisdom is my own:
the Holy Spirit is the Hunter's Deer.

And in the dark in all enchanted lands
I know the Spirit is that Burning Bush
toward which the artist gropes with outstretched hands.

Upon the waters once and then again
I saw the Spirit in a silver rush
rise like the Quarry of the Fishermen.

Yet this I know: no arrows of desire
can wound Him, nor a bright intrepid spear;
He is not seen by any torch of fire,

nor can they find Him who go wandering far;
His habitat is wonderfully near
in each soul's thicket 'neath its deepest star.

Let those who seek come home through the vain years
to where the Spirit waits a shining captive.
This is the hunt most worthy of all tears.

Bearing their nets celestial, let them come
and take their Quarry on the fields of rapture
that lie beyond the last gold pendulum.

(1934)

Celestial Bird

O sweet and luminous Bird,
Having once heard Your call, lovely and shy,
I shall be hungry for the finished word.
Across the windy sky

of all voiced longing and all music heard,
I spread my net for Your bewildering wings,
but wings are wiser than the swiftest hands.
Where a bird sings

I held my heart, in fear that it would break.
I called You through the grief of whip-poor-wills,
I watched You on the avenues that make
a radiant city on the western hills.

Yet since I knew You not, I sought in vain.
I called You Beauty for its fleet white sound.
But now in my illumined heart
I can release the hound

of love upon whose bruising leash I strain.
Oh, he will grasp You where You skim the sod,
nor wound Your breast, for love is soft as death,
swifter than beauty is, and strong as God.

                    (1928; 1946)

Lo Spirito Santo

The Spirit of God
is wind and water,
fire and a bird.
Substance and sod,
earth and matter
have formed one word.

For who has looked
on a fire blowing
and has not seen
banners erect
and waves going
and a bird lean
on a shoulder of wind?

And who has stood
near a sea burning
under the blind
sun's eye and could
by no thought's turning
look on fire,
or a wind racing,
or a bird thrown
higher and higher
toward towers facing
the sea, toward stone?

So beauty's bird,
wind-wisdom seeking,
and sorrow's flood,
and love's flame stirred,
are one voice speaking
a word called God.

For Fire a word
with light its daughter
(and their golden Breath),
name for a Bird
and wind and water
that have no death.

(1929; 1939; 1945)

Ruah-Elohim

Spirit in Hebrew, feminine in gender,
lifts my surmise to touch sweet certainty
that with a goodness like maternity
the Holy Ghost is tender.

Master and guide suppose a separation
should native weakness contravene their role,
but in event of mothering in the soul
hope fondles all creation.

Not as the newest infant who is bringing
no more than burden, I would to Him
yearling in grace and with the cherubim,
say all my love by clinging.

The elders must take conflict and distraction
from how and who and whither and the rest;
but always for children carried at the breast
love is the lone exaction.

Two are the Son and Father, but the Other
so shapes my will its dear theology.
Come but to kiss and cradle tenderly
is Love Who seeks to mother.

(1954)

Decoys

Make decoys he told me,
set them on the blue;
then observe the wild ducks
flying down to you.

Wild ducks do not charm me
save for beauty's sake.
But decoys of Spirit—
these I strain to make.

The decoy of silence,
hope's unuttered sigh,
that the Ultimate Silence
drift down from the sky.

The chaste dovelike virtue,
whiteness to allure
One Who is a Spirit,
infinitely pure,

Love's decoy, the fire bird
that, when God shall see
the Winged Flame of heaven
may come down to me.

Let him have his wild ducks,
green and blue and brown.
My decoys are fashioned
to bring heaven down.

(1951)

The Spirit's Name

Dove is the name of Him and so is Flame,
and Love can push aside all eager symbols
to be His peerless and His proper name.
And Wind and Water, even Cloud will do,
if it is heart that has the interview.

But when at last you are alone with Him
deep in the soul and past the senses' choir,
Oh, give Him then that title which will place
His unpredictable breath upon your face:
O Dove, O Flame, O Water, Wind, and Cloud!
(And here the creature wings go veering higher)
O love that lifts us wholly into God!

O Deifier.

(1955)

Night of Storm

The times are winter. Thus a poet signed
our frosty fate. Life is a night of snow.
We see no path before us, nor behind;
Our faithless footprints from our own heels blow.
Where can an exile out of heaven go,
with murk and terror in a trackless place
and stinging bees swept down upon his face?

Or what is else? There is your world within.
and now the soul is supplicant: O most
wretched and blind, come home! Where love has been
burns the great lantern of the Holy Ghost.
Here in His light, review your world of frost:
a drifting miracle! What had been night
reels with unending eucharists of light.

(1939)

Come, South Wind

"By south wind is meant the Holy Spirit who awakens
love."

St. John of the Cross

Over and over I say to the south wind: come,
waken in me and warm me!
I have walked too long with a death's chill in the air,
mourned over trees too long with branches bare.
Ice has a falsity for all its brightness
and so has need of your warm reprimand.
A curse be on the snow that lapsed from whiteness,
and all bleak days that paralyze my land.

I am saying all day to Love who wakens love:
rise in the south and come!
Hurry me into springtime; hustle the winter
out of my sight; make dumb
the north wind's loud impertinence. Then plunge me
into my leafing and my blossoming,
and give me pasture, sweet and sudden pasture.
Where could the Shepherd bring
his flocks to graze? Where could they rest at noonday?
O south wind, listen to the woe I sing!
One whom I love is asking for the summer
from me, who still am distances from spring.

(1954; 1984)

To Live with the Spirit

To live with the Spirit of God is to be a listener.
It is to keep the vigil of mystery,
earthless and still.
One leans to catch the stirring of the Spirit,
strange as the wind's will.

The soul that walks where the wind of the Spirit blows
turns like a wandering weather-vane toward love.
It may lament like Job or Jeremiah,
echo the wounded hart, the mateless dove.
It may rejoice in spaciousness of meadow
that emulates the freedom of the sky.
Always it walks in waylessness, unknowing;
it has cast down forever from its hand
the compass of the whither and the why.

To live with the Spirit of God is to be a lover.
It is becoming love, and like to Him
toward Whom we strain with metaphors of creatures:
fire-sweep and water-rush and the wind's whim.
The soul is all activity, all silence;
and though it surges Godward to its goal,
it holds, as moving earth holds sleeping noonday,
the peace that is the listening of the soul.

(1949; 1984)

Love

The Little Nation

Having no gift of strategy or arms,
no secret weapon and no walled defense,
I shall become a citizen of love,
that little nation with the blood-stained sod
where even the slain have power, the only country
that sends forth an ambassador to God.

Renouncing self and crying out to evil
to end its wars, I seek a land that lies
all unprotected like a sleeping child;
nor is my journey reckless and unwise.
Who doubts that love has an effective weapon
may meet with a surprise.

(1941; 1946)

In This Green Wood

I found my Truelove
in this green forest
one sacred midday.
(My heart believes
though dawn and evening
are wholly hallowed,
none match a midday
with lighted leaves.)

The trees were steeped in
great brews of sunlight.
No leaf was stirring
from floor to sky.
How looked my Truelove?
What said my Truelove?
No dearest language
could testify.

Love closed its gateway.
Seek not to enter
but pass by humbly
as creature should.
I here tell all that
my heart could utter:
I found my Truelove
in this green wood.

The Flower of Love

"Where there is no love, put love and you will find love."
—St. John of the Cross

Whoever first plants the seed in any soil
hitherto fallow,
and cultivates the shoot with humble toil
near steep or shallow—

They will be first to come upon the flower
whose instant glory
can recreate, in even this trivial hour,
the Eden story.

Blessed are they who stand upon their vow
and are insistent
that love in this bleak here, this barren now
become existent.

Blessed are they who battle jest and scorn
to keep love growing
from embryo immaculately born
to blossom showing.

Primarily for them will petals part
to draw and win them.
It, when the pollen finds their opened hearts,
will bloom within them.

(1948)

Cabaret

I shall spend a penny of love,
and a penny of grief,
And a penny for song,
wine that is red, wines that are purple and white;
I shall find a place in the dazzling room of life,
and sit on a chair and sip my wine all night.

Dancers will come like red and gold leaves blown
over a crystal floor, and I shall see
many a reveller wander out alone
through a black door beyond all revelry.

There will be music come on little feet
into my soul, and laughter to be spread
over young wounds, and kisses honey-sweet,
and shining words to keep me comforted.

And I shall wait till the Keeper comes to say
that my hour is done, and he drowns each glaring light
in endless black . . . and the dancers go away . . .
and I stumble out alone into the night.

(1926)

Letter of Departure

"There is nothing in the valley, or home, or street
                              worth turning back for—
nothing!" you write. O bitter words and true
to seed the heart and grow to this green answer:
let it be nothing to us that we knew
streets where the leaves gave sparsely of the sun
or white small rested houses and the air
strung with the sounds of living everywhere.
The mystery of God lies before and beyond us,
so bright the sight is dark, and if we halt
to look back once upon the burning city,
we shall be paralyzed by rage or pity,
either of which can turn the blood to salt.

We knew too much of the knowable dark world,
its secret and its sin,
too little of God. And now we rise to see
that even our pledges to humanity
were false, since love must out of Love begin.
Here where we walk the fire-strafed road and thirst
for the great face of love, the blinding vision,
our wills grow steadfast in the heart's decision
to keep the first commandment always first.
We vow that nothing now shall give us cause
to stop and flounder in our tears again,
that nothing—fire or dark or persecution—
or the last human knowledge of all pain—
shall turn us from our goal.

With but the bare necessities of soul—
no cloak or purse or scrip—let us go forth
and up the rocky passes of the earth,
crying, "Lord, Lord," and certain presently
(when in the last recesses of the will
and in the meshes of the intellect

43

the quivering last sounds of earth are still)
to hear an answer that becomes a call.
Love, the divine, Love, the antiphonal,
speaks only to love,
for only love could learn that liturgy,
since only love is erudite to master
the molten language of eternity.

(1941; 1946; 1969; 1984)

My Heart Ran Forth

My heart ran forth on little feet of music
to keep the new commandment.
(O feast and frolic of awakening spring!)
It would beguile the world to be a garden
with seeds of one refrain: *My little children,*
love one another; so my heart would sing.

But wisdom halted it, out far afield,
asked: did you sow this seed
around your house, or in the neighbor's garden
or any nearby acreage of need?
No? Then it will not grow in outer places.
Love has its proper soil, its native land;
its first roots fasten on the near-at-hand.

Back toward the house from which I deftly fled,
down neighbors' lanes, across my father's barley
my heart brought home its charity. It said:
love is a simple plant like a Creeping Charlie;
once it takes root its talent is to spread.

(1948; 1984)

I Hold My Heart As A Gourd

I hold my heart as a gourd filled with love,
ready to pour upon humanity,
not that I see each one as my own neighbor
though veiled with strangeness or with enmity,
and not that it is my own self I see,
my sins and virtues and my secret mind
multiplied almost to infinity.
Though this to love a proper cause might be,
not in these words is my true love defined.

I hold my heart as a gourd ready to pour
upon all those who live.
Not that I see each one as come from God
and to my soul His representative,
but that God inhabits what He loves
and what His love sustains, and hence I see
in each soul that may brush against my soul
God Who looks out at me.

(1942; 1946)

The Rock Too High for Me

Up toward the rock too high for me, too tall
for my small reach, I clambered, but in vain.
I was cast down to sober earth again.

Who would believe me if I cared to tell
that Love wrought this undoing, that Love's hand
dashed me from heights, then kindly offered me
wit to have peace in shadows where I stand?

Who would believe me if I said that grace
devised this lodging in a lowly place?

Though bathed in an immeasurable forgiveness,
a blinding love that wakes the furthest trust,
yet I am Moses straining his eyes on Pisgah;
I am Job, stopping his mouth with ashes;
I am Jeremiah, face in the dust.

(1987)

This Paltry Love

I love you, God, with a penny match of love
that I strike when the big and bullying dark of need
chases my startled sunset over the hills
and in the walls of my house small terrors move.
It is the sight of this paltry love that fills
my deepest pits with seething purgatory,
that thus I love you, God—*God*—who would sow
my heights and depths with recklessness of glory,
who hold back light-oceans straining to spill on me, on
me,
stifling here in the dungeon of my ill.
This puny spark I scorn, I who had dreamed
of fire that would race to land's end, shouting your
worth,
of sun that would fall to earth with a mortal wound
and rise and run, streaming with light like blood,
splattering the sky,
soaking the ocean itself, and all the earth.

(1984)

Come Is the Love Song

Come is the love song of our race and Come
our basic word of individual wooing.
It lifts audacious arms of lowliness
to majesty's most amiable undoing,
to Godhood fleshed and cradled and made least.
It whispers through closed doors a hurry, hurry
to Tierce and fiery feast.
The liturgy of Advent plucks its bud
from the green shrub of love's compendium:
O Wisdom, Adonai, Root of Jesse
and sign by which the mouths of kings are dumb,
O Key, O Orient, King and Cornerstone,
O our Emmanuel, come.
And Paschaltide prepares an upper room
where burns the fuller bloom.
Come is the small sweet-smelling crib we carve
from fir and bear across December frost.
It is the shaft of the flame-hungry Church
in Paschal spring, or the heart's javelin tossed
privately at the clouds to pierce them through
and drown one in the flood of some amazing
personal Pentecost.

(1952; 1984)

I Would Define My Love

Here on the flyleaf of the garish day,
here at the noonday of my long despair
I write the grave inconsequence of words.
When men stampede in panic-stricken herds
down tangled roads of thought,
speech dies without the seal of action there,
and even song, cast forth, must come to naught,
lost in the blowing pockets of the air.

Shall I then sit apart in a sun stupor
out of the rush of the bewildered feet
and fan my heart to keep it fresh and cool,
and say, "O beautiful. . ." and say "O sweet. . .",
watching the butterflies that try to settle
on wet leaves in a water-lily pool?

No, for my heart is on the road with these
spiritual refugees,
and I would flee the grim inaction of words
and the paralysis of wish and dream.
How can a man in love sit and stare?
O people of earth, if I am not with you, running
    and crying,
it is that I am paging hurriedly
through wordless volumes of reality
to find what love has indicated there.
I would define my love in some incredible penance
of which no impotent language is aware.

(1941; 1984)

Encounter of Love

Downfalls of goodness on her barren life
brought peaks of praise. She stood on the cool ledge
of Lauds and made her total melody
effective answer. But the rains came on
in shameless mercy and her throat went dry.
Silence alone could wear the reverence
that dares to worship. Once, in too much light,
she glanced aside and saw her inch of worth,
a mind too small, a heart too small where sky
and land and even soil and refuse shone.
Then even silence died, pauper and fool.
Nothing but pain could go to meet such love.

The Gift of Love

My thoughts of you are fair as precious stones
out of the memory's deep mysterious mines.
I cut and polish, hold the gems to light—
color of sea water, color of wines
coaxed from the earth's sweetest fruits. I drop them
                                                    down
into my heart, into the lifted hands
of love whose lone concern is your renown.

Heaven

The Homecoming

The spirit, newly freed from earth,
is all amazed at the surprise
of her belonging: suddenly
as native to eternity
to see herself, to realize
the heritage that lets her be
at home where all this glory lies.

By naught foretold could she have guessed
such welcome home: the robe, the ring,
music and endless banqueting,
these people hers; this place of rest
known, as of long remembering
herself a child of God and pressed
with warm endearments to His breast.

(1984)

Manuscript of Heaven

I know the manuscript the Uncreated
writes in the garden of His good estate.
His creatures are the words incorporated
into love's speech. O great

immortal Poet, in Your volume bright
if one may choose a portion, write me down
as a small adjective attending light,
the archangelic noun.

(1938)

Heaven

The gates of heaven are an allegory
and only symbol shapes its guarded door,
nor does the soul plunge headlong into glory
without a rumor of a light before.

Though God, indeed, has reservoirs of morning
whose unguessed joy we distantly extol,
yet word and choice are altering and adorning:
heaven is something happening in the soul.

(1951; 1984)

The Cloud of Carmel

"The Lord promised that He would dwell in a cloud."
—(2 Chronicles 6:1)

Symbol of star or lily of the snows,
rainbow or root or vine or fruit-filled tree:
these image the immaculate to me
less than a little cloud, a little light cloud rising
from Orient waters cleft by prophecy.
And as the Virgin in a most surprising
maternity bore God and our doomed race,
I who bear God in the mysteries of grace
beseech her: Cloud, encompass God and me.

Nothing defiled can touch the cloud of Mary.
God as a child willed to be safe in her,
and the Divine Indweller sets His throne
deep in a cloud in me, His sanctuary.
I pray, O wrap me, Cloud, . . . light Cloud of Carmel
within whose purity my vows were sown
to lift their secrecies to God alone.
Say to my soul, the timorous and small
house of a Presence that it cannot see
and frightened acre of a Deity,
say in the fullness of your clemency:
I have enclosed you all.
You are in whiteness of a lighted lamb wool;
you are in softness of a summer wind lull.
O hut of God, deepen your faith anew.
Enfolded in this motherhood of mine,
all that is beautiful and all divine
is safe in you.

(1946)

56

Total Virgin

"She was virgin even of herself."—Pere Francois, O.C.D.

In a house of mirrors that coveted her image
she never walked
with her own beauty
nor made a feast of her goodness,
inviting friends from the far and wide.
She never sat down with her own innocence
to dialogue together,
nor called a stranger in
to sit at her hearth and be glorified.

She was a maiden promised to one lover
whom she was always seeking.
Though he hid in her heartbeat and settled himself
behind her breath,
he was distance, too. Journeys dwindled to places
beside her own, and miles melted beneath
her steps of wanting. She could by-pass all
meadows that trap us with their poisonous flowers
and their soliciting pools
and winding lanes that skirt the only death.

She was out on a road alone, hastening onward,
gathering all as gift, the small and great
fragments of mystery and reality.
Everything was for Him, even her own being.
Since love marks neither measurement or weight
she carried all, without touching or tasting.

Life which comes as a virgin to us all,
most safely came to her.
Time, when she passed, remained inviolate.

(1976; 1984)

Young Maidens Running

(For the novices)

Saint I defined for you: a slow serene
candle in a cathedral solitude,
a virgin lily in a nameless wood.

Yet you are flowers of petalled fire that lean
on a swift wind or waves that ride the sea
in tender rushings toward divinity.

O living phrases from the Canticle!
I sing you, maidens that arise and run
in the stained footsteps of the King's young Son.

Hence must I now for saint a new concept tell:
a maiden racing toward a sole desire
with garments glowing and her face on fire.

(1955)

The Blood's Mystic

Grace guards that moment when the spirit halts
to watch the Magdalen
in the mad turbulence that was her love.
Light hallows those who think about her when
she broke through crowds to the Master's feet
or ran on Easter morning,
her hair wind-tumbled and her cloak awry.
What to her need were the restrictions of
earth's vain formalities?
She sought, as love so often seeks and finds,
a Radiance that died or seemed to die.

One can surmise she went to Calvary
distraught and weeping, and with loud lament
clung to the cross and beat upon its wood
till Christ's torn veins spread a soft covering
over her hair and face and colored gown.
She took her First Communion in His Blood.

O the tumultuous Magdalen! But those
who come upon her in the hush of love
claim the last graces. A wild parakeet
ceded its being to a mourning dove,
as Bethany had prophesied. We give
to Old Provence that solitude's location
where her love brooded, too contemplative
to lift the brief distraction of a wing.
There she became a living consecration
to one remembering.
Magdalen, first to drink the fountained Christ
Whose crimson-signing stills our creature stir,
is the Blood's mystic. Was it not the weight
of the warm Blood that slowed and silenced her?

(1950)

The Book of Ruth

The dedicated of the Blessed Mother
discover their prefigurement in Ruth.
They dwell in Moab, in a pagan darkness
of sinfulness and self,
a country never colonized by truth.
The Son of Mary who had found and claimed them
departed by a death within the senses.
They stood bewildered in a plundered youth.

Where could they go? They chose the new Noemi,
her people and her God, the distant strange
land of the spirit, higher Israel.
Her soul's kept sun destroyed their inner cloister
of night; they took horizons in exchange.
Known mode gave way to the abstruse and alien
design of life her counsels might arrange.

What was the end then of their self-donation:
the Mother's wisdom, deep and esoteric,
became their prod.
She bade them seek, in faith's chaste, reverent darkness
Him Who is slumbering with His Heart awake,
Who is by mercy mystically unshod.
The Godhead is the soul's eternal Lover.
By grace of their alliance with her Son
she bade them creep up humbly and uncover
the feet of God.

(1948)

Night Prayer: To the Prophet Elijah

This is the edge of time; this cliff encounters
the valleys of the measureless unknown
and the great surges of those outer seas
where swim Orion and the Pleiades.
I like to come here in the night alone.

I like to seek this arched and alien window,
lean into night and lift my restless love
to pastures where an ancient prophet tethered
horses of fire. I cry, "My father, my father,
the chariot of Israel and the driver thereof!"

Where dwells this lonely eremite I know not,
hid by what torrent, by what ravens fed;
but when the moon suggests his solitude,
my mind has taste of an unearthly food;
where the night shines, my heart is visited.

He who was swept by fire to time's suspension,
yet to be slain and in the judgment tried—
is he not closer to our human pity
than those who triumph in a lasting city,
the far impassible beatified?

Here I touch space that borders the eternal;
here, undistracted by the clock's poor rhyme,
I stand, an emigrant of earth whose place
is nearer heaven, being near to grace,
and hold my heart out, over the sill of time.

(1947; 1984)

The Granite Woman

The hour she enters hush your lovely song.
She has no road for velvet-slippered feet;
her mind that bore earth's agony so long
would crumble underneath a load so sweet.

Her heart that shut its doors on love's wide calling
that was as granite where the storms begin,
would break beneath the weight of petals falling
out of the music of this violin.

(1929)

The Pool of God

There was nothing in the Virgin's soul
that belonged to the Virgin—
no word, no thought, no image, no intent.
She was a pure, transparent pool reflecting
God, only God.
She held His burnished day; she held His night
of planet-glow or shade inscrutable.
God was her sky and she who mirrored Him
became His firmament.

When I so much as turn my thoughts toward her
my spirit is enisled in her repose.
And when I gaze into her selfless depths
an anguish in me grows
to hold such blueness and to hold such fire.
I pray to hollow out my earth and be
filled with these waters of transparency.
I think that one could die of this desire,
seeing oneself dry earth or stubborn sod.
Oh, to become a pure pool like the Virgin,
water that lost the semblances of water
and was a sky like God.

(1950; 1984)

And in Her Morning

The Virgin Mary cannot enter into
my soul for an indwelling. God alone
has sealed this land as secretly His own;
but being mother and implored, she comes
to stand along my eastern sky and be
a drift of sunrise over God and me.

God is a light and genitor of light.
Yet for our weakness and our punishment
He hides Himself in midnights that prevent
all save the least awarenesses of Him.
We strain with dimmed eyes inward and perceive
no stir of what we clamored to believe.
Yet I say: God (if one may jest with God),
Your hiding has not reckoned with Our Lady
who holds my east horizon and whose glow
lights up my inner landscape, high and low.
All my soul's acres shine and shine with her!
You are discovered, God; awake, rise
out of the dark of Your Divine surprise!
Your own reflection has revealed Your place,
for she is utter light by Your own grace.
And in her light I find You hid within me,
and in her morning I can see Your Face.

(1945; 1946)

About Bruno

Saint Bruno's gift was his uninterrupted
conversation with God.

How did this wonder come to him? Without
Carthusian insights I can only guess:
there must have been at first some seeds of grace
which Bruno planted in his wilderness.
He must have watered them with tears, and kept
his little garden friendly to the sun
till the shoots came and, marvelously, flowers.
(Words were his flowers, to woo the Holy One.)
Bruno had peace, I know, but all the same
I doubt that he perceived if answers came.

And surely there were winters in his heart
when leaf and blossom died, and the land froze,
and a white silence covered everything.
He offered God this silence, I suppose,
and his cold poverty (which few believe
that God in His warm silence will receive).

How did this wonder come at last to him?
I would surmise: when Bruno understood
how love that crushed him had no gift for God—
though through all seasons he had sought the good—
he entered his own hut, pulled down the shades,
and sat and grappled with his pain till he
himself became the word, the total need,
the gift, the outcry, the last agony.
And one day God, most ready to discover
the moment that a heart fills to the brim,
burst into Bruno's time, sat down beside him,
and eager with delight gave to this lover
the joy of endless dialogue with Him.

(1984)

65

Abraham

I love Abraham, that old weather-beaten
unwavering nomad; when God called to him,
no tender hand wedged time into his stay.
His faith erupted him into a way
far-off and strange. How many miles are there
from Ur to Haran? Where does Canaan lie,
or slow mysterious Egypt sit and wait?
How could he think his ancient thigh would bear
nations, or how consent that Isaac die,
with never an outcry nor an anguished prayer?
I think, alas, how I manipulate
dates and decisions, pull apart the dark,
dally with doubts here and with counsel there,
take out old maps and stare.
Was there a call at all, my fears remark.
I cry out: Abraham, old nomad you,
are you my father? Come to me in pity.
Mine is a far and lonely journey, too.

(1967; 1984)

The Visitation Journey

The second bead: scene of the lovely journey
of Lady Mary, on whom artists confer
a blue silk gown, a day pouring out Springtime,
and birds singing and flowers bowing to her.

Rather, I see a girl upon a donkey
and her too held by what was said to mind
how the sky was or if the grass was growing.
I doubt the flowers; I doubt the road was kind.

"Love hurried forth to serve." I read, approving.
But also see, with thoughts blown past her youth,
a girl riding upon a jolting donkey
and riding further and further into the truth.

Angels

In a Cloud of Angels

I walk in a cloud of angels.
God has a throne in the secret of my soul.
I move, encircled by light,
blinded by glowing faces,
lost and bewildered in the motion of wings,
stricken by music too sublime to bear.
Splendor is everywhere.
God is always enthroned on the cherubim,
circled by seraphim.
Holy, holy, holy,
wave upon wave of endless adoration.
I walk in a cloud of angels that
            worship Him.

Like the Bright Seraphim

Like your bright brothers seraphim
who veil their faces with their wings,
you hide your face, and yet I know
that when the pinions stir and blow
you peer at God and me and things.

I love those glances of your soul,
so shyly sent. I stand aside
and watch, with deeper pleasurings,
the hidden face behind the wings,
a *Sanctus* waiting to be cried.

Ah, guard this native secrecy!
Know, child: those angels chief in grace
who stir when Splendor breathes His Name
and wake and slumber in His flame
alone use wings to hide their face.

(1956)

Ministering Spirits

Never go anywhere without the angels
who watch God's face and listen to be sought.
Greater than you, yet they have joy to serve you.
Never go blundering through the jungle, thought,
without a clear-eyed one to part the branches,
shout snake or swamp-hole, cry a rock beware.
The angels of the Lord encamp around you
in any place you pitch your tents for prayer.

Know that your soul takes radiance from the angels.
She glories in these creatures of her kind
and sees herself thus lightsome, free as wind.
She stands abashed when the flesh rudely brings
its homage to these pure intelligences
and tries to crowd their beauty into bodies
and weight their grace with gravity of wings.

(1951; 1984)

Michael

Michael is a prince of God and page of Mary.
He stands beside the tall throne of his Queen.
He is the warrior who made peace in heaven
and keeps the earth serene.

Then why should I take fright when foes or demons
assail me with their treacheries or wrath,
when I have knowledge that the Queen's archangel
is keeper of my path?

O heart, believe. The great winged prince of heaven
watches the Queen's child with a warrior's eye
and lifts his flaming spear and comes like lightning
at the first cry.

(1947)

Beauty, Too, Seeks Surrender

Love writes surrender as its due;
but how is beauty actor?
The heart remembers wound and loss
while mind sings benefactor.

God takes by love what yields to love,
then pours a glowing allness
past the demolished walls and towers
into the spirit's smallness.

God's beauty, too, surrender seeks
and takes in the will's lull
whatever lets itself be changed
into the beautiful.

And so, Michelangelo
has marked it out to be,
since beauty is the purging of
all superfluity,

The yielded soul that lifts its gaze
to harms past nature's claim
expects to have experience
of blade and file and flame.

(1952)

The Evening Chimes

Music ingathers all, yet takes one only
into its secret when the chimes begin.
When that great rain of sound comes down, the lonely
of spirit is elect and enters in.
Our evening shines with bells; alone, apart,
we listen, awed,
to the antiphonal pealing of our hearts.

Music by right is for the solitaries
whom a long silence trains to the profound.
The bells are ours; we come at the first airy
rumor to drench our deserts with their sound.
Yet anyone who listens may become
hermit or anchorite under that shower
when the great chimes-tree shakes its leaves of light.

At Sunset

Night after night these sunsets spread their thrill,
confound me in my dreaming for an hour.
I lift my mind in wonder to the power
of color glorified by light until
I know the miracle each western hill
sees when the scattered clouds come into flower—
petals of shining roses and a shower
of flushed gold falls, and my wild heart is still.

Now for a time the soul is visible,
luminous wings lift out on either side
and I am faint who house this beautiful
gold bird; my clouds of thought are glorified.
Color and light possess me. I am one
with stars and moonlight and the dying sun.

Place of Ruin

There must be some place darker to the eye
than this gray shack above a cluttered walk.
Burdocks are green though all the grass is dry,
and still beneath these eaves the swallows talk.

There must be some place without any beauty,
favored of God, as with reproof of pain,
bleaker than stalks in some forgotten garden
under a winter rain.

There must be some house from which even a poet
would hide her frightened face,
where God, grown weary of the brush of beauty,
has used the burning pencil of His grace.
O come and take my hand, you whom I love,
and let us find that place.

(1939)

Siesta in Color

Near a glazed window drinking south and west
in thirst of sunlight in the early spring,
I with a sudden luck of illness take
magic siesta. I commune with color,
hobnob with rainbows on the coasts of slumber,
revisit prisms of long disregard.

Soft pinks, impetuous yellows splash the wall
and line my eyelids as I drift toward sleep;
blue, green and aqua prance in patterns; purple
and lavender to squares and circles run.
I think if I could track this charm to source
or else to terminal I might discover
opening or dropoff or amazing shore
to color's primal meaning.
                              Yet I muse:
is not pure fact a fullness? I remember
how rainbows had addressed me as a child,
how light and color made their language heard.
Though I was not yet judge or analyst,
something secure was given, kept; I held,
as with my grandmother's warm bursts of Gaelic,
sweet words that had no meaning but were there.

(1970; 1984)

Gaelic Music

No one is here to guard me from this music
which sets itself to lilting in the heart.
I run with it, away from commonplaces,
from ditto marks called days and frequent faces.
Where does it go, that gay and nameless road
down which our frolics start?

Certainly not toward rule. Nor yet, indeed,
toward indecorum. I have found its like
in books and pictures fair with the unknown.
I half suspect we pass reality,
and yet this strangeness makes a home for me
and takes me as its own.
I ask and ask, but no one ever tells me
what place we go when I meet Gaelic music
and we are left a little while alone.

Liturgical Seasons

O Full of Lilies

Easter to me my little sister is,
and I affirm her April's eminence.
No beauty of atoning penances
prevails on light as does her innocence.

Our abstract night is into day transmuted
when she makes entrance into any room.
A call goes out to sunrise, April fluted.
Wakened in dew, the Easter lilies bloom.

Wide rumor says that she must dine on light
to show such health of it in her clear face.
The concept of the flowers is also right
with gleam implicit in the scent of grace.

O full of lilies in the time of lovers!
My little sister whom night did not mar
wins Easter first; its luster, one discovers,
favors the gardens where the lilies are.

(1956; 1984)

In Too Much Light

The Magi had one only star to follow,
a single sanctuary lamp hung low,
gold ornament in the astonished air.
I am confounded in this latter day;
I find stars everywhere.

Rumor locates the presence of a night
out past the loss of perishable sun
where, round midnight, I shall come to see
that all the stars are one.

I long for this night of the onement of the stars
when days of scattered shining are my lot
and my confusion. Yet faith even here
burns her throat dry, cries: on this very spot
of mornings, see, there is not any place
when the sought Word is not.
Under and over, in and out, this morn
flawlessly, purely, wakes the newly born.
Behold, all places which have light in them
truly are Bethlehem.

(1964)

The Hidden Christ

I went into the Christmas cave;
there was no Child upon the straw.
The ox and ass were all I saw.

I sought His stable where He gave
His goodness in the guise of bread.
Emptiness came to me instead.

Filled with my Father's words, I cried
"Where have You hid Yourself?" and all
the living answered to my call.

I found Him (and the world is wide)
dear in His warm ubiquity.
Where heart beat, there was Christ for me.

I went back to the Christmas cave,
glad with the gain of everywhere.
And lo! the blessed Child was there.

Then at His feasting board He gave
embrace. He multiplied His good
and fed in me the multitude.

(1963)

Advent

I live my Advent in the womb of Mary.
And on one night when a great star swings free
from its high mooring and walks down the sky
to be the dot above the *Christus i*,
I shall be born of her by blessed grace.
I wait in Mary-darkness, faith's walled place,
with hope's expectance of nativity.

I knew for long she carried me and fed me,
guarded and loved me, though I could not see.
But only now, with inward jubilee,
I come upon earth's most amazing knowledge:
someone is hidden in this dark with me.

(1948)

Michigan Boulevard, Chicago

There is a star above this street for me.
Hither I came of old,
bearing my myrrh and frankincense and gold.

Hunger and loneliness and poverty
I brought for their delight
once in my youth upon a snowy night.

I did not follow to the inmost place
where the Child lay asleep.
It was too splendid; the light dripped too deep.

I saw the tears upon the Virgin's face.
I gave my gifts to her,
and the night ended in a golden blur.

(1932)

Green Is the Season

Green is the season after Pentecost.
The Holy Ghost in an abstracted place
spreads out the languid summer of His peace,
unrolls His hot July.
O leaves of love, O chlorophyll of grace.

Native to all is this contemplative summer.
The soul that finds its way through Pentecost
knows this green solitude at once as homeland.
Only the heart, earth held and time engrossed,
dazed by this unforeknown and blossoming nowhere,
troubles itself with adjectives like "lost."

(1954)

The Song of Distance

Little One, come, I will teach you the song of distance
whereby to flee this peacelessness and din.
Turn from the earth as stranger and begin:
    My soul is out on paths that have no ending
    and no return. Where the noon kneels to pray
    love guides my steps, ascending and descending.
    Out through the sleeping solitudes I stray
        O far
            O far away.
Morning and evening do not mark this day.

O Little One, believe that earth is alien.
Let its concerns all unremembered lie.
Say to the storm or sweetness passing by:
    My soul is out on paths that have no ending
    and no return. A light blurs out my way.
    I am with God and toward my godhood tending.
    I near the foothills of eternal day
        O far
            O far away.
God speaks to me. Earth has no more to say.

III.
The Human Journey: The Agony and the Ecstasy

Creaturehood: Our Poverty and Aloneness

Counsel for Silence

Go without ceremony of departure
and shade no subtlest word with your farewell.
Let the air speak the mystery of your absence,
and the discerning have their minor feast
on savory possible or probable.
Seeing the body present, they will wonder
where went the secret soul, by then secure
out past your grief beside some torrent's pure
refreshment. Do not wait to copy down
the name, much less the address, of who might need you.
Here you are pilgrim with no ties of earth.
Walk out alone and make the never-told
your healing distance and your anchorhold.
And let the ravens feed you.

(1951; 1984)

There Is a Homelessness

There is a homelessness, never to be clearly defined.
It is more than having no place of one's own, no bed or
   chair.
It is more than walking in a waste of wind,
or gleaning the crumbs where someone else has dined,
or taking a coin for food or clothes to wear.
The loan of things and the denial of things are possible
   to bear.

It is more, even, than homelessness of heart,
of being always a stranger at love's side,
of creeping up to a door only to start
at a shrill voice and to plunge back to the wide
dark of one's own obscurity and hide.

It is the homelessness of the soul in the body sown;
it is the loneliness of mystery:
of seeing oneself a leaf, inexplicable and unknown,
cast from an unimaginable tree;
of knowing one's life to be a brief wind blown
down a fissure of time in the rock of eternity.
The artist weeps to wrench this grief from stone;
he pushes his hands through the tangled vines of music,
   but he cannot set it free.

It is the pain of the mystic suddenly thrown
back from the noon of God to the night of his own
   humanity.
It is his grief; it is the grief of all those praying
in finite words to an Infinity
Whom, if they saw, they could not comprehend;
   Whom they cannot see.

                              (1946; 1984)

The Moment After Suffering

Time's cupped hand holds
no place so lenient, so calm as this,
the moment after suffering. It is like
a sunlit clearing after densest wood,
bright by antithesis.
One sits upon a stump to get one's bearing
and to admire such evidence of day.
Thicket and tangle fade; the furtive creatures
of darkness take their leave and slink away.
One feeds upon a succulent rich wisdom
that, to the mind's surprise, has naught to do
with late abjection; it is revelation,
God-fathered, heaven-new.

Oh, there are woods, of course, long forest stretches
of wide inhabited darkness to be crossed,
with pain and hunger, fear of unnamed creatures,
an imminent certainty of being lost.
But even these elude this meditation,
or if intrusive bring yet more release.
One muses as to what it will be like
to step at last from final forest into
the infinite meadows of unending peace,
a place all light and yet not lighted by
the harsh, obtrusive sun that walks our sky,
light that the soul assimilates until
not witness but participant it stands,
taking of Godhead its amazing fill.

(1949; 1984)

Creature of God

That God stands tall, incomprehensible,
infinite and immutable and free,
I know. Yet more I marvel that His call
trickles and thunders down through space to me;

that from His far eternities He shouts
to me, one small inconsequence of day.
I kneel down in the vastness of His love,
cover myself with creaturehood and pray.

God likes me covered with my creaturehood
and with my limits spread across His face.
He likes to see me lifting to His eyes
even the wretchedness that dropped His grace.

I make no guess what greatness took me in.
I only know, and relish it as good,
that I am gathered more to God's embrace
the more I greet Him through my creaturehood.

The Soul That Cries to God

The soul that cries to God out of the hot heart
   of contrition
is indisputably heard.
Here is the pact of love; it is triply signed
   with a sure eternal seal.
Though the whimpering call creeps out from the
   den of the coiled serpent
that hides from God and lies in wait for the
   Virgin's heel,
it stirs a sudden hastening out of heaven
to the place of the cry. God takes this piteous one
   at its urgent word.
He bundles it into His ship, with all its holdings,
and the island of sin is left behind,
   in distance blurred.
And He who redeems will use for the soul
the full extent of its cargo:
the songs, the memory's trivia, the sweet or acid tears,
the spoils or the debt of frightening arrears.
Ingenious to save, in the end His love
   will put to divine advantage
   the wisdom (if wisdom could be the word) of the wasted
   years.

                    (1948; 1984)

The Masses

My love had not the openness to hold
so cumbersome a human multitude.
People in bulk would turn the dials of my heart to
Cold.
The mind would bolt its doors and curtly vow
to leave the crowded streets for a while.
And yet if there were patronage in heaven
my passion was to be
mother of the masses, claiming by some small right of
  anguish
this piteous and dear humanity.
Out of its need my heart began devising
ways to receive this breathing populace
without the warm oppression of its weight,
and the fastidious mind sought out as good
a multiplicity of motherhood
till the reluctant answer entered late:
I learned from God the ancient primal mother
whose hunger to create has brought forth these,
a multitude in lone nativities,
whose love conceived the numberless, and none
by twos and thousands; and with Him I bear them
in separate tenderness, one by one.

(1947)

If You Have Nothing

The gesture of a gift is adequate.
If you have nothing: laurel leaf or bay,
no flower, no seed, no apple gathered late,
do not in desperation lay
the beauty of your tears upon the clay.

No gift is proper to a Deity;
no fruit is worthy for such power to bless.
If you have nothing, gather back your sigh,
and with your hands held high, your heart held high,
lift up your emptiness!

(1940; 1946; 1984)

Humility

Humility is to be still
under the weathers of God's will.

It is to have no hurt surprise
when morning's ruddy promise dies,

when wind and drought destroy, or sweet
spring rains apostatize in sleet,

or when the mind and month remark
a superfluity of dark.

It is to have no troubled care
for human weathers anywhere.

And yet it is to take the good
with the warm hands of gratitude.

Humility is to have place
deep in the secret of God's face

where one can know, past all surmise,
that God's great will alone is wise,

where one is loved, where one can trust
a strength not circumscribed by dust.

It is to have a place to hide
when all is hurricane outside.

(1947; 1984)

Israel Again

Here I am, Israel dragging home from battle
with neither horse nor soldier at my side.
Where are the troops with which I sallied forth
and all the bright insignia of my pride?
I did not call on the Lord God of Hosts,
but rushed forth in my strength to meet the foe.
Here I lag home, a spectacle of wounds,
stripped of my armor, moaning as I go.

When will you learn, O witless Israel,
that he who clings to God in his distress
wins with the weapons of his nothingness?

I step outside myself in gay derision
to mock this torn one, but in sympathy.
I add, "Not all is lost! Oh, turn and see!
Borne after you by the divine forgiveness
is the rich booty of humility."

(1950)

Richer Berry

Now that the bright red berries lend
color to the June berry tree
my need is urgent to befriend
denial and austerity.

I touch the fruit with lips of wish
and with the fingers of soft words,
and leave them, a delicious dish
in taste and substance, to the birds.

From break of bloom till tide of frost
summer has feasts on every hand
spread with no evidence of cost
for any pilgrim to demand.

Yet I can see through wisdom's eyes
how when the first harsh cold begins,
she takes all fruit and merchandise
save what is stored in memory's bins.

No husk, no shell after the rich
full fruit shall dull my later day.
I shall take hunger first, on which
the spirit thrives best, anyway.

(1939; 1946)

This May Explain

The door to God, the door to any grace
is very little, very ordinary.
Those must remember who would gain the place
this rule that does not vary:
all truth, all love are by humiliation
guarded, as One has testified before.
This may explain why the serf finds salvation,
and kings and scholars pass the little door.

(1946)

On Reading Saint Peter of Alcantara

Go alone, he says, to the land of the living,
barefooted, poor,
saluting no one. On this bleak way only
are your steps secure.
Enter in by the gate humility,
his word admonishes, and there embrace
the chill and sharpness of a lonely place.
What are you, nothingness before the All,
and you cling to self as to your good
and spurn your God to keep your creaturehood.
This is the season of the soul's undoing,
the terrible gateway into the profound,
and it is less a penitent's renewing
than entrance, birth and difficult beginning.
Lights focus on the years of waste and sinning,
and in God's presence shame has depths to sound.
Take off your shoes here; it is holy ground.

Yet this is earth; to reach the pure white valley
a way must burn through continents unknown.
Drive yourself forth, O love so newly born,
by blandishment or scorn.
Set out, O soul, in darkness and alone.
You are too feeble yet to bear the leaning
of any other soul, too poor to feed
the smallest mouth of humanity in its need.
It is by flight alone that you are freed.
Go forth then without speech or salutation
and make your borders peace. Admit no ill
into your emptied heart, for in aloneness
God speaks; He names His way where all is still,
and what He hollows out His mercies fill.
Earth has no calm to parallel the soothing
of wanting only the eternal Will.
How glorious, O soul, is this your journey!
Love is its end and love its plan and prod.
Set out then in the riches of your nothing.
Enter into the solitudes of God.

(1946)

Without Beauty

The spirit travels unmolested
once she has measured beauty's worth
nor weeps to see herself divested
of every comeliness on earth.

The body may grow poor and charmless,
and age inscribe its added jest.
The mind may stand, a not too harmless
buffoon in its own blunders dressed.

The troublous heart that hurried after
each silly windfall of no gain
may starve and die. Lament and laughter
now ply their crafty trades in vain.

Unloveliness becomes her treasure
whom God's attraction pleases well.
She is His contrast and His pleasure
whose beauty captured her from hell.

And though she walks in rags and tatters,
her face is to a sunset turned.
And what she has no longer matters
before this light that she has learned.

For God within her stoops to sharing
the splendor that is His alone
which still were hid had she come bearing
one spurious beauty of her own.

(1946)

No One Can Stay

Though you be lined with down,
or though you be enameled with new light,
O tender moment that I now disown,
still will I pass you in the swirling night.

Your invitation is with fraud extended,
and you will say, once I have come to rest:
the frost has come; the season of gain is ended;
rich as you are, you cannot be my guest.

No one can stay
in any golden moment, and no more
will I let any trick of light betray
me to a house that is nothing but a door.

(1939; 1984)

For a Child of God

The saints and mystics
had a name
for that deep
inwardness of flame,
the height or depth
or ground or goal
Which is God's dwelling
in the soul.

Not *capax Dei*
do you say;
nor yet
scintilla animae
nor *synderesis*—
all are fair—
but heaven,
because God is there.

All day and when
you wake at night
think of that place
of living light,
yours and within you
and aglow
where only God
and you can go.

None can assail you
in that place
save your own evil,
routing grace.
Not even angels
see or hear,
nor the dark spirits
prowling near.

But there are days
when watching eyes
could guess that you
hold Paradise.
Sometimes the shining
overflows
and everyone
around you knows.

(1953)

The Great Mystery

My uncle had one sober comment for
all deaths. Well, he (or she)
has, he would say, solved the great mystery.
I tried as child to pierce the dark unknown,
straining to reach the keyhole of that door,
massive and grave, through which one slips alone.

A little girl is mostly prophecy.
And here, as there before,
when fact arrests me at that solemn door,
I reach and find the keyhole still too high,
though now I can surmise that it will be
light (and not darkness) that will meet the eye.

(1984)

Los Angeles Earthquake

There was a mystery abroad that night.
I, too, was restless in my bed; I turned
and tossed. Dreams spilled debris across my sleep,
trapped me in rubble, hemmed me in with ruin
not too unlike what San Fernando Valley
yielded at sunrise. How could my just wrath
fall on that restless giant lain still so long,
shifting for arm's ease or a shoulder rest,
soothing a muscle spasm or a foot
asleep, or racked by some disordered dream?

I wonder was he seeing what I saw:
not too much left of time which out at sea
was sinking and with none to rescue her?
Or of his waking eye did he discern
how soon the sands run out for both of us?
Anyway, he turned over and his weight
of bedding moved with him, and houses fell.

If I could find him, wakeful still with pain,
harried by dreams, discomfited by fear,
I think that I could reassure him now:
new earth, new heaven. See, the end is sweet.
My brother, sleep. You'll need your whole great strength
for later rising in some glorious dawn.

(Editors' note: earthquake in San Fernando Valley,
2/9/1971; 69 people died.)

Escape

I have escaped from fear and loneliness
when this great city's dusk descends on me.
It is a childhood's game of make-believe,
filched from the years in my necessity.

I think: if I should open this dark door,
I could step into roadways lined with clover,
take the wind's merchandise of down and scent,
and have the whole starred sky of home for cover.

I think: if I would lift this window now
and pause to listen, leaning on this sill,
I might hear, for my heart's full consolation
the whip-poor-wills on some Wisconsin hill.

Petenwell Rock

I never shall forget the first gay night
I came for dancing here;
Out of a long black road there bloomed this bright
portion of revel, near
a tall pine-wreathed rock, as certain as a wall.

Out of the night suddenly lights had mellowed
to warm young gold glistening against a hall
where dancers swayed like songs, and music bellowed
its anger against grief; and laughter flying
fell on my ears like sounded waterfall.

But overhead the whip-poor-wills were crying,
crowding all loneliness into one cry,
and a great rock maintained a wise old silence,
lifting its strength into a starlit sky.

O silver loneliness!
        O golden laughter!
O grief that only loneliness should last!
Madness will die, and youth will hurry after.
Into some shadowed past
dancers will bow like dust; laughter will crumble,
while still beneath the silver of the moon
for loveliness and joy that died too soon
these plaintive birds will cry,
and this tall rock will watch with calm indifference,
holding itself aloof against the sky.

(1926)

103

Old Bridge

Here is the bridge my childhood marked with fear.
I thought an ogre waited under it,
quick to devour if I should venture near.
I ran at sight of it; my sandals hit

the brown dust of the roadway going by.
Oh, it was like a day of lifted dread
when I grew bold enough to peer and pry,
seeking the monster, finding peace instead.

Fled is that childish fear; my thoughts are couched
in grown-up wisdom now, and yet I find
that worse than ogres are the dark shapes crouched
lurking beneath the bridges of my mind.

(1939)

The Monk at Quadragesima

Come, death.
Walk in this season of your grim renown.
Come, let me have my bouts with you, knave
who tracked my Master down.

I honor you with shares of all I have.
Break bread with me; be sated at my table.
Snatch your sweet portions of my scanty rest.
Take all that I am able
to give of all that flesh and blood keep bringing
when cosmic bells have set my senses ringing.
Eat your cold way into my self-esteem
till even the deep subtle root has died.
Wrest from my mind the crowns of which I dream.
Take the externals; take the bright inside.
Tear out impatience by the handfuls—so.
Grab, if you can, my pride
and thieve those words that leave me deified.
Come death, my friend, my friend.
I know the good your coming works in me.
Shape me to Christ before my journey's end;
Hack me and hew me till Christ comes to be
my dear identity.

For certainly I know
that in our sharp encounter well I fare.
With you as guest beside me all is gain.
You slay me, death, but then I rise to live
and you yourself are slain.

(1956)

Suffering

All that day long I spent the hours with suffering.
I woke to find her sitting by my bed.
She stalked my footsteps while time slowed to timeless,
tortured my sight, came close in what was said.

She asked no more than that, beneath unwelcome,
I might be mindful of her grant of grace.
I still can smile, amused, when I remember
how I surprised her when I kissed her face.

(1965)

One Answer

Downfalls of goodness on her barren life
brought peaks of praise. She stood on the cool ledge
of lauds and made her total melody
effective answer. But the rains came on
in shameless mercy and her throat went dry.
Silence alone could wear the reverence
that dares to worship. Once, in too much light,
she glanced aside and saw her inch of worth,
a mind too small, a heart too small where sky
and trees and even soil and rubbish shone.
Silence cried out and crumbled at her feet.
Nothing but pain could go to meet this love.

(1965)

Obscurity

Obscurity becomes the final peace.
The hidden then are the elect, the free.
They leave our garish noon and find release
in evening's gift of anonymity.

Lost, not in loneness but in multitude,
they serve unseen without the noise of name.
Should you disdain them, ponder for your good:
it was in this way that the angels came.

(1952; 1984)

Renunciation

"To compose the most sublime poetry is of less worth
than the least act of self-renunciation."
                                    —St. Therese

Let the rapt poet with his dulcet art
this finer rhythm heed.
Past plodding iamb, dancing anapest
here is a lyric of the absolute
for genius to create or scholar hold—
book to the light—and read.

Those walking toward the angels always rise
from sound to silence; the harmonious soul
goes outward from the discord of the senses,
lays down the tasted and the spoken word
and is made whole
by the unsavored, the inaudible.
Secret to ears of earth yet loud in heaven
is this pure music, rhythm's utter gain.
As we approach God and as we hear
its soundless cadences, our hungers strain
to sate themselves on metaphors of suffering
and new melodious similes of pain.

(1948)

The Book and the Cup

I am reading out of the book of my own evil;
I am drinking out of the cup of my own shame
here in the darkness with no candle lit.
The Hand of God is holding the book for me,
and I am reading it.
He is holding the cup and its drink is liquid flame.

Where can I hide from this vast condemnation?
The Face of God is merciful, is kind;
yet my own script is pitiless to accuse,
and the deep draught of my own conscience sears.
I try, as once, to make escape through weeping;
but here one sees more clearly through one's tears.

Oh, to be lost, destroyed, obliterated!
To have the self in me erased and done!
Would I were naked spirit holding God
and all else nothingness, oblivion. . .

Yet since the Will of God presents this book,
I would not turn from it to look upon
the fairest poetry that earth has given.
I would not trade this cauterizing cup
for all the wines in heaven.

(1947)

For a Proud Friend, Humbled

In that least place to which all mercies come
I find you now, settled in peace, at home,
poor little one of Yahweh. On your face
only response of love lies, with no trace
or drifting hint of what had brought you low.
Down steps of like unworthiness I go
weighted with heart (and how heart can oppress!)
to see you humbled into gentleness
(and into innocence) so utterly.
Pray me, my blessed, into your company.

(1970; 1984)

The Leftovers

With twenty loaves of bread Elisha fed
the one hundred till they were satisfied,
and Scripture tells us there was bread left over.
Jesus did more: with five small barley loaves
and two dried fish he fed five thousand men,
together with their wives and children, all
neatly arranged upon the cushioned grass.
The awed disciples, when the crowd had eaten,
gathered up what was left: twelve baskets full.

Who then received these fragments? Hopefully,
the least (though not less favored) and the poor.
I think of those who always seem to get
the leavings from the banqueting of others,
the scraps of bread, of life, that goodness saves.
I pray that they come proudly when invited,
make merry at their meal and have their fill,
and rise up thankfully, remembering
the fragments, too, were miracles of love.

(1986)

Human Winter

No fire could warm this place
though the air hang in sultry shred and the roof
perspire;
nothing here is amenable to fire.

Words fall in slow icy rain and freeze
upon the heart's sudden dismantled trees,
and branches break and fall.
From the wind of inclement glances I cannot shield
myself
who find their frost too subtle to forestall.
I am waiting for the snow of my own obscurity to settle
and cover me, frozen ground,
to blunt all sharp insufferable sound,
to meet the angles of cold and obliterate them all.

I long to rise in this room and say, "You are not my
people,
I come from a warm country; my country is love.
Nor did I wish to come here; I was misdirected."
But their frost is not defied and their cold is not rejected.
So chilled am I by this presence of human winter
I cannot speak or move.

(Editors' note: this poem was written before Jessica
Powers entered Carmel; written in 1939 or 1940;
published in 1942).

I Measure Loneliness

I measure loneliness,
spreading the tape from chime to evening chime,
and it is taller than the sky's blue stress
and lengthier than time.

* *

None spreads the tape with me.
The music of the bells alone is guide.
I had not thought that loneliness could be
so infinitely wide.

* *

I cross the plains, the ocean with its spangles,
the cloud-impaling mountains and I own
that still my measuring tape obscurely dangles
out into the unknown.

* *

It is at this
moment of bells that I most clearly know
time's measures all are fraud and artifice.
No one on earth could mark the miles I go.

Awake at Night

Dread of the dark: a straggler, a last bird
snatches his final feasting in last light,
then off to where the black arms of the forest
open to welcome in his leaping love.
A small one in the predatory night
tumbles to trustful slumber on a bough.
I, sheltered and secure,
but with late news making a heavy bedclothes,
lie wakeful: fear says to my lumpy pillow
do not in any circumstances conform.

Draw Me: We Will Run

Draw me, the spouse sang; draw me; we will run.
And morning enters here; a secret sun
bursts from the skyline of the pronoun *we:*
all whom I love I bear by grace with me.
I carry them, sweet burden, as I go
up through the mountain darkness, through the slow
labored ascents. No goal is set too far
if where I am, my heart's elected are.
No cliff cries halt between me and their good
beyond. And the propitious likelihood
that I can sanctify myself for them
inspires each new ascetic stratagem.
O God, my Hive, protect me as I come,
a laden bee bearing its treasure home.

Old Woman

None walks so wise as self, so enterprising
to shift earth's precious best to her own need.
She is like some old crone that time has sharpened
to find the succulent fruit on which to feed
the wood for fuel. And she would never be
concerned that love might be a thievery.

They speak the old man in us; I find, rather,
a shrewd old woman bustling in my mind,
with woman's trickeries and subterfuges
to confiscate what her caprices find.
This is the way I make my gifts to heaven:
I follow her; I watch her and I stand
ready to wrest her treasures from her hand.
I marvel at her methods to outwit me,
her ingenuity, her self-command.
For even when I rob her utterly
she goes and makes a little feast of pleasure
out of a woe she calls humility.

The Tear in the Shade

I tore the new pale window shade with slightly
more than a half-inch tear.
I knew the Lady would be shocked to see
what I had done with such finality.
I went outside to lose my worry there.
Later when I came back into the room
it seemed that nothing but the tear was there.

There had been furniture, a rug, and pictures,
and on the table flowers in purple bloom.
It was amazing how they dwindled, dwindled,
and how the tear grew till it filled the room.

I Do Not Touch You

Beautiful is this tree with its glossy leaves,
with Pentecost still playful in its branches.
I do not touch it with inquiring hand
nor break off fiery bloom to shout hosanna in my window,
nor wrench it up to root again, gay as pageant in my land.
Let it stand.

You whom I love I do not touch with even a dreamed
    possession
nor is this poem for you; I carry it past
your open door in a basket of secrecy.
I do not point you out as loved, nor speak about you or
    to you
save, out of hearing, once, that lone imperative
of all true lovers: be.

I leave you here in the innocence of your being,
joyful and unpossessing.
My claiming, out of time, will dearer be.
And innocence, that concentrate of peace,
spreads like the haze of a soft summer noon
and encircles me.

Journey of the Soul

The Soul Is a Terrible Thing

The soul is a terrible thing; it cannot die.
Though it run past the heart's beat and the lung's breath
and cry through all the valleys of endlessness
it cannot find its death.

The soul is a terrible thing, and it has only
one of two destinies:
up steeps of light that to the eye below
are too remote, too lonely,
cliffs of negation where the heart's herb withers,
solitudes chilled and barren, or a deep
unknown where midnight wanders in her sleep.
Yet its ascensions open upon wonder,
plateaus of midday, balconies of sun,
and its last peak can cleave the white air under
the firmament called God, the final One.

Failing to rise, the soul can turn and follow
the way of its own willing and be lost,
crossing somewhere the boundaries of love,
that safe sweet nation of the Holy Ghost.
The soul though born of God can yet be given
to ultimate evil and be one of those
in pain alone preserved
whom the apt metaphors of Judas enclose:
wandering stars to whom the storm of darkness
is forever reserved.
Yet its true destiny confounds all language,
even the mind's profound imagined word
For on the heights of grace it yet may be

the secret chamber of a Deity
where what is spoken in God, in God is heard.
And What is Love proceeds eternally,
possessing utterly.

Oh, at this mystery that lies within me
I walk indeed with trembling, or I stand
crying God's pities out of His right hand—
that I, so poor a creature, am so favored
with this too precious gift of soul, that I
bear in so undependable a vessel
this terrible, terrible thing they call a soul.

(1945; 1946)

The House at Rest

On a dark night
  Kindled in love with yearnings—
  Oh, happy chance!—
  I went forth unobserved,
  My house being now at rest.

—St. John of the Cross

How does one hush one's house,
each proud possessive wall, each sighing rafter,
the rooms made restless with remembered laughter
or wounding echoes, the permissive doors,
the stairs that vacillate from up to down,
windows that bring in color and event
from countryside or town,
oppressive ceilings and complaining floors?

The house must first of all accept the night.
Let it erase the walls and their display,
impoverish the rooms till they are filled
with humble silences; let clocks be stilled
and all the selfish urgencies of day.

Midnight is not the time to greet a guest.
Caution the doors against both foes and friends,
and try to make the windows understand
their unimportance when the daylight ends.
Persuade the stairs to patience, and deny
the passages their aimless to and fro.
Virtue it is that puts a house at rest.
How well repaid that tenant is, how blest
who, when the call is heard,
is free to take his kindled heart and go.

(1984)

The Place of Splendor

Little one, wait.
Let me assure you this is not the way
to gain the terminal of outer day.

Its single gate
lies in your soul, and you must rise and go
by inward passage from what earth you know.

The steps lead down
through valley after valley, far and far
past the five countries where the pleasures are,

and past all known
maps of the mind and every colored chart
and past the final outcry of the heart.

No soul can view
its own geography; love does not live
in places open and informative.

Yet, being true,
it grants to each its Raphael across
the mist and night through unknown lands of loss.

Walk till you hear
light told in music that was never heard,
and softness spoken that was not a word.

The soul grows clear
when senses fuse: sight, touch and sound are one
with savor and scent, and all to splendor run.

The smothered roar
of the eternities, their vast unrest
and infinite peace are deep in your own breast.

That light-swept shore
will shame the data of grief upon your scroll.
Child, have none told you? *God* is in your soul.

                                    (1945; 1946; 1984)

Wanderer

(from the *Scivias* of St. Hildegarde)

Where did I dwell? I dwelt in the shadow of death,
as did a mystic anciently aver.
Where did I walk? I walked on the primitive
pathway of error, was a child of earth
(and down the years my speech betrayed my birth).
What did I hold for ease against my breast?
The flimsy comfort of a wanderer
for whom there is no rest.

Two nestlings vied for life in me: I fed
the greedy one whose talent was to beg
(no one had warned me of the cowbird's egg).
I let the little one grow thin and pale
and put a blame on life that she was frail.

How did I ever come then to the light?
How did I ever, blind with self, discover
the small strict pathway to this shining place,
I who betrayed the truth over and over,
and let a tangle of dark woods surround me?
Simple the answer lies: down cliffs of pain,
through swamps and desert, thicket and terrain,
oh, Someone came and found me.

(1979; 1984)

The House of the Silver Spirit

I am a February child. I love these things—
This broken shell of a house and the terrible song it
sings.
And winter shrieking wildly at this door.
It has been here for eighty years or more.

With Mile Bluff on the west and on the east
Sheep Pasture Bluff, it spreads a lavish feast
for sound as any singer dreams to do.
Out on the frosted highway of the wind
its roofs are honed, its walls are razor-thinned
till winter sweeps an icy river through.

I think this house broke from some wild travail
when Indian wigwams made this placid dale
a place of haunting treachery and dread,
and copper faces lifted up to see
this strange new miracle that came to be.
I think at first it was untenanted
like clay that waits the coming of a soul.
And when the wintry tides began to roll
over these roofs the silver spirit came.
From the unholy wind it learned the song
that pleased its bitter mouth these ages long,
a song that trembles like a frosty flame.

I do not know how wisdom entered it,
suddenly as the cold white stars are lit
or slowly like a window-spread of frost.
I only know that I have failed to trace
the lives that crumpled in this barren place.
Here they were born and here gave up the ghost;
if they are not still here, then they are lost.

I came to birth here in a month of snows,
and it is only winter my mind knows—

the incantation of wailing pines,
the hills in moonlight etched in frostly lines,
the cold lamenting of the whip-poor-wills.

House of my frozen hope, on you I fed,
dreamed at your window, wept upon your bed
through the long shivery years of white and blue.
And till I die and after death has passed
your singing soul will hold my spirit fast
with silver threads of winters that I knew.
Oh, even now the needle pushes through—

There was one winter of a dreadful lack:
the wolves howled all night in the tamarack
swamps in the moonlight; they had dared so near
this house; and my mind's house, a whole age younger,
cried with the wolves the same wild ache of hunger,
a sound more deep and terrible than fear.

There was a winter when I took a breath
for the first time from the white fields of death,
(always on nakedness the cold would press)
till in surrender I became a cry,
a tone in this bright building's lullaby.
Some other child shall swallow my distress,
hear in these walls my echoing loneliness.

Therefore, my music, you must never be
fragile and sweet and a profanity;
Let all my tones be clear and sharp and wild.
This old house bore me in her frosty womb
and winter cradled me in sound and gloom;
I am their desolate and frightened child.

("a great deal of poetic exaggeration in this poem"
—Jessica Powers)

(1937)

126

The Variable Heart

This was her heart till now; a milkweed seed
anchored securely to a wisp of down.
It had a drifting desultory creed;
but love remained its verb, remained its noun.

Think how the wind moved and tormented her
and cast her forth on rock, or arid clay,
how even the least gust prevented her
from any constancy save her dismay.

This is a garden: pray the wind may let
her down in that soil where her roots can move.
Ask God to hold her till her roots are set
safe in the windless moment of His love.

(1940; 1946)

Enclosure

Gypsy by nature, how can I endure it—
This small strict space, this meager patch of sky?
What madness once possessed me to procure it?
And deed it to myself until I die?

What could the wise Teresa have been thinking
to set these bounds on even my little love?
This walling, barring, minimizing, shrinking—
how could her great Castilian heart approve?

And yet I meet the morrow with composure.
Before I made my plaint I found the clue
and learned the secret to outwit enclosure
because of summits and a mountain view.

You question, then, the presence of a mountain?
Yet it is here past earth's extravagant guess—
Mount Carmel with its famed Elian fountain,
and God encountered in its wilderness.

Its trails outrun the most adept explorer,
outweigh the gypsy's most inordinate need.
Its heights cry out to mystic and adorer.
Oh, here are space and distances indeed.

(1948)

Return of the Victor

No song can make a wreath for this dark brother
who spent his strength upon an unseen thrust,
who spread his beauty for the tide to smother
rather than put to sea with the unjust.

There was no war, no wound in sight of goal,
no bomb or shell, no falling plane ablaze,
save in the inmost places of the soul
where the grim siege can be prolonged for days

without a mortal witness. Earth makes little
of battles fought for strange democracies
when her towers fall and all her bones are brittle.
She wars enough within her boundaries.

So homeward turns this victor, his war ended.
Down a dull road with weary steps and slow
he struggles on, unsung and unattended.
And it is fitting that this should be so.

(1938; 1939; 1984)

On Reading a Perfect Poem

This is the place long coveted, long sought,
immaculate and cold.
This is the upper region of pure thought
where Eden's lost integrities unfold.
I climb up toward a mountaintop of snows
where a white mass of untouched blossom blows,
I see the virgins following the Lamb
whatever way He goes.

(1946)

The Far Island

Heaven to me a mystic Erin is,
God's sea-encircled dwelling, wholly lit
by its own inner and eternal day,
and all my birds of longing nest in it.

I pray to Patrick of the Trinity
to gain for me this isle of the Triune.
Grant me to turn my prow into its port
before the cycle of the next new moon.

I pray to Brigid, Mary of the Gael,
so clothe me with the Virgin it may be
that when my mantle sweeps against the waves
they may take heed to her tranquility.

Brendan the Voyageur I too implore:
through these dark waters take me to my goal.
As once you found my earthland, find for me
the unimagined homeland of my soul.

Have pity, saints of Erin; help my ship
out to the blessed isle! And till I be
anchored in God my postexilic Good,
O Columbkill the exile, pray for me.

(1946)

The Books of Saint John of the Cross

Out of what door that came ajar in heaven
drifted this starry manna down to me,
to the dilated mouth both hunger given
and all satiety?

Who bore at midnight to my very dwelling
the gift of this imperishable food?
my famished spirit with its fragrance filling,
its savor certitude.

The mind and heart ask, and the soul replies
what store is heaped on these bare shelves of mine?
The crumbs of the immortal delicacies
fall with precise design.

Mercy grows tall with the least heart enlightened,
and I, so long a fosterling of night,
here feast upon immeasurably sweetened
wafers of light.

(1939)

132

The Second Giving

The second giving of God is the great giving
out of the portions of the seraphim,
abundances with which the soul is laden
once it has given up all things for Him.

The second growth of God is the rich growing,
with fruits no constant gathering can remove,
the flourishing of those who by God's mercy
have cut themselves down to the roots for love.

God seeks a heart with bold and boundless hungers
that sees itself and earth as paltry stuff;
God loves a soul that cast down all He gave it
and stands and cries that it was not enough.

(1946)

The Terminal

It was Fifth Avenue, and it was April.
Who could have dreamed such wind and flying snow?
The terminal gleamed gold far in the distance.
And then I thought: where truly do we go?

Is it not thus we wander out of time
down the bright canyons of white whirling air,
too cold and tired for beauty, and too sad
to utter secrets that are warm to share?

Some nights were meant for tears, and some for
laughter;
and some to hold in trust, and some to spend.
But portents were astir that night we sighted
the terminal that stands at the world's end.

(1939)

Track of the Mystic

There was a man went forth into the night
with a proud step. I saw his garments blowing;
I saw him reach the great cloud of unknowing.
He went in search of love, whose sign is light.
From the dark night of sense I saw him turn
into the deeper dark nights of the soul
where no least star marks a divine patrol.

Great was his torment who could not discern
this night was God's light generously given,
blinding the tainted spirit utterly
till from himself at last he struggled free.
I saw him on the higher road to heaven:
his veins ran gold; light was his food and breath.
Flaming he melted through the wall of death!

(1932; 1939)

One Time as a Child

One time as a child on the rim of creation
I walked into the area left by the sun.
The house that I lived in by distances dwindled,
and the earth rolled away like a top that was spun.

I climbed out of my body and wandered and wandered
through the fabulous meadows that constitute sky.
The clouds like some great colored snowdrifts were
   shoveled
to the east of the path I was travelling by.

The last thing I saw on the earth was a church spire
in the city of Mauston below me and far.
I stopped at the gate of the silver-blue seamen
who teach the young west how to anchor a star.

I came back from my journey so clean and so shining
that no matter what dark fell I still would be free.
I climbed into my body out back of the pine trees,
and night drifted down over Mauston and me.

(1946; 1984)

Yes

Yes to one   is often no to another
here walks my grief   and here has often been
my peak of anguish   yes is the one need
of my whole life   but time and time again
law forces no   up through my heart and lips
spiked leaden ball   rending as it arises
leaving its blood and pain   yes is the soft
unfolding of petals   delicate with surprises
curve and caress   and billowing delight
out to the one or many   I would guess
heaven for me   will be an infinite
flowering of one species   a measureless sheer
beatitude of yes

(1984)

Millet's "Feeding Her Birds"

Millet the artist has provided me
with all I ask for in biography.

These children and the mother and a bowl—
here is the scene which circumscribes my soul.

Fledglings of peace whose need is their defense—
these are my insights into innocence.

I would be one of them; if wish be heard,
this round one leaning forward like a bird,

her hands behind her and her lifted face
waiting its mouthful. Let my day erase

its wary woe for what she knows of trust,
which is the purest homage of our dust.

Her peasant childhood motivates my will
to take my given portion and be still;

or if there must be words, to speak none other
than: O my Mother God, my God and Mother.

(1984)

("The image of God as Mother comes from Julian of
Norwich." Jessica Powers)

There Shall Come Forth a Shoot

I am waiting for a green shoot
to come out of my stump some morning
in this unseasonal springtime—
December's leaf and blossom, winter's bird.
Joy waits with me and I can feel its seepage
into my day and night.
My bones sing and I hear an unknown music
from that one place where, by old reverence stirred,
the vowels drain from a word.
I think of the marvelous flower that is to come
and how the light will hover over it.
Now and again though is the message blurred
by brief uncertainties:
I fear that by my rude excess of watching
the green may be deterred
or that I have miscalculated seasons
or given far too personal a meaning
to glorious promises Isaiah heard.

Yet who am I to minimize the worth
of what a stump is likely to bring forth?

At Evening with a Child

(For Maureen)

We walk along a road
at the day's end, a little child and I,
and she points out a bird, a tree, a toad,
a stretch of colored sky.

She knows no single word
but "Ah" (with which all poems must commence,
at least in the heart's heart), and I am stirred
by her glad eloquence.

Her feet are yet unsure
of their new task; her language limited,
but her eyes see the earth in joy secure.
And it is time I said:

Let the proud walls come down!
Let the cold monarchy be taken over!
I give my keys to rust, and I disown
castles of stone for ambushed roads in clover.

All the vast kingdoms that I could attain
are less to me than that the dusk is mild
and that I walk along a country lane
at evening with a child.

(1939)

Water and Light

I am reading my holy mother, Madre Teresa.
Dazzled with her clear sight,
I am holding fast to the bannisters of time,
climbing her stairs of light.
Enter this fluid day and climb with me
through what her pages tell:
the soul in the state of grace is like limpid water
out of a crystal well.
I see the light upon my sisters' faces
lifted to God, world over. On these stairs
glory and grace are cloudbursts over me,
out of her soul and theirs.
Have you seen water ever that got tangled
with light and came alive and was divine?
I drown in these torrents out of her soul and theirs,
and (God forgive me) mine.

Star, First Magnitude

The five points of his star are *I, me, mine,*
to me and *for me*, and he shines with these.
The quick mind gasps to see how soon his light
cancels Orion and the Pleiades.
When he begins effectively to shine,
even the Christmas star is put to flight.

He sees his splendor blazing through all darkness,
and there is none within his circle, none
to tell him what his helpless earth will come to
now that he routs the sun.
The trees and flowers of grace go down in frost.
Thus is good love by too much twinkling lost.

Prayer: A Progression

You came by night, harsh with the need of grace,
into the dubious presence of your Maker.
You combed a small and pre-elected acre
for some bright word of Him, or any trace.
Past the great judgment growths of thistle and thorn
and past the thicket of self you bore your yearning
till lo, you saw a pure white blossom burning
in glimmer, then, light, then unimpeded more!

Now the flower God-is-Love gives ceaseless glow;
now all your thoughts feast on its mystery,
but when love mounts through knowledge and goes free,
then will the sated thinker arise and go
and brave the deserts of the soul to give
the flower he found to the contemplative.

(1954)

Prayer

Prayer is the trap-door out of sin.
Prayer is a mystic entering in
to secret places full of light.
It is a passage through the night.
Heaven is reached, the blessed say,
by prayer and by no other way.
One may kneel down and make a plea
with words from book or breviary,
or one may enter in and find
a home-made message in the mind.
But true prayer travels further still,
to seek God's presence and God's will.

To pray can be to push a door
and snatch some crumbs of evermore,
or (likelier by far) to wait,
head bowed, before a fastened gate,
helpless and miserable and dumb,
yet hopeful that the Lord will come.
Here is the prayer of grace and good
most proper to our creaturehood.
God's window shows his humble one
more to the likeness of His Son.
He sees, though thought and senses stray,
the will is resolute to stay
and feed, in weathers sweet or grim,
on any word that speaks of Him.

He beams on the humility
that keeps its peace in misery
and, save for glimmerings, never knows
how beautiful with light it grows.
He smiles on faith that seems to know
it has no other place to go.

But some day, hidden by His will,
if this meek child is waiting still,
God will take out His mercy-key
and open up felicity,
where saltiest tears are given right
to seas where sapphire marries light,
where by each woe the soul can span
new orbits for the utter man,
where even the flesh, so seldom prized,
would blind the less than divinized.

(1951; 1984)

To a Young Wood-Carver

Through the mind's motherhood
you hope to bring
out of this fragrant wood
a new warm thing.

A shepherd, child or elf,
here deftly sought,
will speak your hidden self,
disclose your thought.

Shaping your secret bent,
what you create
becomes your document
or duplicate.

Mind what you say in art.
Here sounds the cry
of that deep privy heart
God judges by.

Nor could the body's child
so well express
how far you were beguiled
toward holiness.

(1956; 1984)

Dreams of You

My dreams of you are like the fallen leaves,
colored with brilliance, nomad rustling things,
tossed by the winds of olden memories—
they prate of golden summertimes and springs.

When skies were gray, you flung them all away—
but I, who loved them, hoard such gifts as these.
By day I revel in their gilded lights;
at night they whisper tender sympathies.

(1924)

147

Only One Voice

Only one voice,
but it was singing
and the words danced and as they danced held high—
oh, with what grace!—their lustrous bowls of joy.
Even in dark we knew they danced, but we—
none of us—touched the hem of what would happen.
Somewhere around a whirl, swirl, a pirouette,
the bowls flew and spilled,
and we were drenched, drenched to the dry bone
in our miserable night.

Only one voice,
but morning lay awake in her bed and listened,
and then was out and racing over the hills
to hear and see.
And water and light and air and the tall trees
and people, young and old, began to hum
the catchy, catchy tune.
And everyone danced, and everyone, everything,
even the last roots of the doddering oak
believed in life.

(1967; 1984)

Covenant

I made a covenant with my hands not to be reaching
for love and praise which once were all my light.
These are for Christ by the most utter right.

I made a covenant with my tongue not to be speaking
of aught that draws me from the Word apart,
much less to interpret Him in my heart.

I made a covenant with my eyes not to be watching
to see what beauty might come down to me.
Christ is my beauty; Him alone I see.

I made a covenant with my heart never and nowhere
to be admitting any lover but Him.
I take for witnesses the seraphim.

This is the document I have been writing
in painful letters for these many years
with shame and failure and a yield of tears.

I made two copies for my own protection:
one to be carried, ready to unroll,
one to post up on gates outside my soul.

The Sign of the Cross

The lovers of Christ lift out their hands to
the great gift of suffering.
For how could they seek to be warmed and clothed
and delicately fed,
to wallow in praise and to drink deep draughts
of an undeserved affection,
have castle for home and a silken couch for bed,
when He the worthy went forth, wounded and hated,
and grudged of even a place to lay His head?

This is the badge of the friends of the Man of Sorrows:
the mark of the cross, faint replica of His,
become ubiquitous now; it spreads like a wild blossom
on the mountains of time and in each of the crevices.
Oh, seek that land where it grows in a rich abundance
with its thorny stem and its scent like bitter wine,
for wherever Christ walks He casts its seed
and He scatters its purple petals.
It is the flower of His marked elect, and the fruit
it bears is divine.

Choose it, my heart. It is a beautiful sign.

(1948; 1984)

The Heart Can Set Its Boundaries

The heart can set its boundaries
on mortal acres without fear.
Descent of skies, cascade of seas
are not to be expected here.

The heart can take a human love
to feed and shelter, if it will,
nor think to see its cities move
in avalanches down a hill.

Only when God is passing by,
and is invited in to stay
is there a split of earth and sky.
Boundaries leap and rush away,

and wound and chaos come to be
where once a world lay, still and small.
But how else could Infinity
enter what is dimensional?

(1941; 1984)

Christ Is My Utmost Need

Late, late the mind confessed:
wisdom has not sufficed.
I cannot take one step into the light
without the Christ.

Late, late the heart affirmed:
wild do my heart-beats run
when in the blood-stream sings one wish away
from the Incarnate Son.

Christ is my utmost need.
I lift each breath, each beat for Him to bless,
knowing our language cannot overspeak
our frightening helplessness.

Here where proud morning walks
and we hang wreaths on power and self-command,
I cling with all my strength unto a nail-
investigated hand.

Christ is my only trust.
I am my fear since, down the lanes of ill,
my steps surprised a dark Iscariot
plotting in my own will.

Past nature called, I cry
who clutch at fingers and at tunic folds,
"Lay not on me, O Christ, this fastening.
Yours be the hand that holds."

(1952; 1984)

Take Your Only Son

None guessed our nearness to the land of vision,
not even our two companions to the mount.
That you bore wood and I, by grave decision,
fire and a sword, they judged of small account.

Speech might leap wide to what were best unspoken
and so we plodded, silent, through the dust.
I turned my gaze lest the heart be twice broken
when innocence looked up to smile its trust.

O love far deeper than a lone begotten,
how grievingly I let your words be lost
when a shy question guessed I had forgotten
a thing so vital as the holocaust.

Hope may shout promise of reward unending
and faith buy bells to ring its gladness thrice,
but these do not preclude earth's tragic ending
and the heart shattered in its sacrifice.

Not beside Abram does my story set me.
I built the altar, laid the wood for flame.
I stayed my sword as long as duty let me,
and then alas, alas, no angel came.

(1956; 1984)

Pure Desert

"The more one runs in the spiritual life
    the less tired one gets."—Padre Pio

This is pure Gobi desert, you declare;
I see, past sandstorms (of exaggeration)
and rage of flesh at ghostly motivation,
pink health invade your prayer.

Pure desert, you complain, though now you walk
who once had shuffled through the arid miles.
Sighting a day of flight, I shelve my smiles
and share your pilgrim talk.

All true ascesis as a desert lies:
hot wind, hot sand, no water, and no way.
The ego agonizes through each day.
Freedom is when it dies.

I coax you onward: soon, first breeze of bliss;
soon, sun that scorches cooled to sun that warms.
Your youth will dance when shady lanes lock arms
with each green oasis.

(1961; 1984)

Having Renounced You

Having tonight renounced you utterly,
and bending low to lay hope in a tomb
that needs no trusty guard lest there be
a subsequent resurrection, making room
across my lands for the long evening,
still have I joy so positive I sing.

For now there is no finger of possession
upon my prayers for you, and when I go
into God's presence with the bleak confession
He will be moved with pity as I stand
holding that master weapon in my hand.

(1938; 1939)

Belmont Harbor

Dusk after dusk here at the harbor found me,
and here I made my choice:
I put the silence that earth spread around me
above the sound of any human voice.

Here I was wed to loneliness made fairer
by youth that watches with its lashes wet.
Ah, slowly the heart learns, and with what error
and what regret!

(1939)

156

Return

This was the fever that beset my years,
that led by pride, I put my aim too high.
I strained my spirit, grasping at the moon;
my heart I wearied, reaching for the sky.

My thoughts like ways and social climbers were
who spurned their childhood home for vistas dim.
I cast the little virtues from my hand
and wrote brief notes to stars and seraphim.

I must come home again to simple things:
robins and buttercups and bumblebees,
laugh with the elves and try again to find
a leprechaun behind the hawthorn trees.

Sign at Sexagesima

I entered the kingdom in Noah's week
at the sign of the rainbow,
out of black waters into the waters of life.
I know my place; I can find my page in the ancient
  Scripture
as all can: prefigurement, a call
to pattern and fulfillment in the new.
With love I bow, with reverence bow before
my sacramental beginnings.

My darkness was always rain and turbulent waters,
a troubled world held in a crowded place.
My light was always rest on a mountaintop
in a new christened innocence of morning
with all the world washed clean.
The earth blushing with youth, dressed herself
in flowers and leaves,
and over all the sign of the sacred rainbow,
covenant like a poem one could read
over and over again and relish meaning,
itself arched doorway and a sudden entrance
to unexpected wisdom and delight.

(1965)

(Editors' note: Jessica Powers reported that she was baptized during Sexagesima week).

The Monastic Song

The theme is penance, poverty the language.
And no luxuriant adverb must come here
to swish its velvet robes, no adjective
save one that is content to meet and marry
with the obscure, the frugal, the austere.
The theme is penance; this is earth, not heaven.
The desert chant demands a solemn note
that would persuade the reverential throat
to naked speech and unembellished phrase.
Love is, of course, admittedly the music:
because of the words of Thy lips I have kept hard ways.
One who would gain this door to preach appeasement
or lay these heavy song-books on their shelves
would but betray us—though by kiss of friendship—
into the hands of our ignoble selves.
Life would be cluttered discord, not the strong
chaste nudity of song.

IV.
Of Birds and Rainbows and All Assorted Things

Nature and Grace

The Valley of the Cat-Tails

My valley is a woman unconsoled.
Her bluffs are amethyst, the tinge of grief;
her tamarack swamps are sad.
There is no dark tale that she was not told;
there is no sorrow that she has not had.
She has no mood of mirth, however brief.

Too long I praised her dolors in the words
of the dark pines, her trees,
and of the whip-poor-wills, her sacred birds.
Her tragedy is more intense than these.

The reeds that lift from every marsh and pond
more plainly speak her spirit's poverty.
Here should the waters dance, or flowers be.

Her reeds are proper symbols of a mother
who from the primer of her own dark fears,
as if the caroling earth possessed no other,
teaches her young the alphabet of tears.

                              (1939)

161

Look at the Chickadee

I take my lesson from the chickadee
who in the storm
receives a special fire to keep him warm,
who in the dearth of a December day
can make the seed of a dead weed his stay,
so simple and so small,
and yet the hardiest hunter of them all.

The world is winter now and I who go
loving no venture half so much as snow,
in this white blinding desert have been sent
a most concise and charming argument.
To those who seek to flout austerity,
who have a doubt of God's solicitude
for even the most trivial of His brood,
to those whose minds are chilled with misery
I have this brief audacious word to say:
look at the chickadee,
that small perennial singer of the earth,
who makes the weed of a December day
the pivot of his mirth.

(1941; 1946)

162

Everything Rushes, Rushes

The brisk blue morning whisked in with a thought:
everything in creation rushes, rushes
toward God—tall trees, small bushes,
quick birds and fish, the beetles round as naught,

eels in the water, deer on forest floor,
what sits in trees, what burrows underground,
what wriggles to declare life must abound,
and we, the spearhead that run on before,

and lesser things to which life cannot come:
our work, our words that move toward the Unmoved,
whatever can be touched, used, handled, loved—
all, all are rushing on *ad terminum*.

So I, with eager voice and news-flushed face,
cry to those caught in comas, stupors, sleeping:
come, everything is running
                    flying,
                          leaping,
hurtling through time!
                    And we are in this race.

(1970; 1984)

Wisconsin Winter

Climate, declared a holy man, can be
a purification;
climate, atonement for the sins of all.
Taken with love, or even resignation,
it can make potent pleading for God's grace.

Snowflake and snowdrift, ice and icicle,
frost on the wall, frost on the windowpane,
frost when my breath edges a scarf with lace:

These are the coins of silver we collect
for others and ourselves. It well may be
that this year will yield fortunes we can pour
into the treasury.

Gifts can be multiplied at mercy's word:
fire for the heart's chill, light for the mind's eye,
a reddened stove to warm a dismal room,
a little lamp to comfort and illume,
even a sun to hang in someone's sky.

When we send greetings on a snow-scene card
or gift at Christmas, will we not wonder whether
there might be more than wishful words to find:
a sunrise, maybe, for the inmost mind;
for deepest heart, some Arizona weather?

For a Lover of Nature

Your valley trails its beauty through your poems,
the kindly woods, the wide majestic river.
Earth is your god—or goddess, you declare,
mindful of what good time must one day give her
of all you have. Water and rocks and trees
hold primal words born out of Genesis.

But Love is older than these.

You lay your hand upon the permanence
of green-embroidered land and miss the truth
that you are trusting your immortal spirit
to earth's sad inexperience and youth.
Centuries made this soil; this rock was lifted
out of the aeons; time could never trace
a path to water's birth or air's inception,
and so, you say, these be your godly grace.
Earth was swept into being with the light—
dear earth, you argue, who will soon be winning
your flesh and bones by a most ancient right.

But Love had no beginning.

Souvenir, Wisconsin River

Mindful of you by love, I think to send you
token of this enchantment that I see
when v-shaped sparkles dance on wind-rushed water
in the sun's path. Insanities of glee
delight when light here, there and everywhere
shines, disappears, re-shines—a fantasy
no words could capture save in small wild fragments
of   v
   v   v
 v   v   v
   v   v
      v

Red Moon

Round-faced papoose,
cradled in black wool clouds,
what holds your thoughts so still—
hunting and battle scars?
Or does your small mind reach
no further than the wind
that cradles you into rest
on a tree of stars?

Wigwams

When the dead white mists
creep up in evening rain,
out of the half-blurred swamp
the ghostly cities rise:
wigwams like gulls' wings spread,
hundreds across a plain;
and I look out on them
through my grandmother's eyes.

The Valley of My Childhood

The valley of my childhood was simple and full of peace,
a young girl sleeping
in a green dirndl dress,
smocking of hedges and flung skirts of grain,
a shining belt of creek thrown loose
in careless slumber.
Or more, my valley was a green quatrain
framed by horizons, where a child might read
a land and water language saved from prose.
The creek was our joy; we pushed our naked toes
into its kissing clearness where the minnows
ran up the scale of silver in their flight.
The clam pretended not to be one of us
and drew his doorway tight.
Sometimes along the willowed shore we startled
the wary killdeer and wading crane.
There was a spring that bubbled its pure sand
into our hands; we lay, hot after running,
and sucked the water up
out of its cold incessancy and ran again.
Off toward the north we sought the virgin meadows
where wild strawberries grew
and moss was a plushy wisdom to our feet.
From his swaying pulpit a bobolink tinkled a near
injunction to his summer-cloistered mate.
We never went further than the pools of cat-tails
where the water said wait.

Meadows curved to the east and tumbled into marshes
where spring was a boom of frogs, fairer than music
since it was close to the creating breath
which had not yet gone home
from the wild water and inviolate ground.
Now and then the evening chilled when a loon
shivered its cry. The night awoke in sound
of whip-poor-will woe; we listened under the moon
to a far cry, tried to unravel distance
and set it down, an owl or a raccoon.

Bluffs horizoned the south. Beneath the shade
of the proud cliques of trees, the fern and shrub
and the wet bark entangled us with odors,
primeval fragrance, washing us from time.
Caves in the rocks were dark and mystery made.
The wonder of what might be hid in there
past the illegible tracks could charge the air.
Where the woods thinned we found the berry patches,
gathered the large soft berries, filled our mouths with
    sweet.
We carried them home in the heat
through woods less friendly now, murmurous with
mosquitoes,
filled with known windings that prevented up
from bright familiar plain.
Our pails and hands wore souvenirs of stain.

This was my valley till a garish sun
exposed it, and a more obtrusive thing
laid searing hands on all its blossoming.
I grew up to reverse the Midas legend:
gold at my touch became, in ruthless day,
something inferior to yellow clay.
Only of late have I gone back to my valley
and by a higher path that parallels
the canceled lanes of old simplicities.
I have found cool equivalents of these
in far green places of a deeper rest.

Stopped by this utmost gain, the long complaining
dies in my throat. No more can I aver
that it would have been better for all of us—
my people and me and the valley that I loved—
if we had stayed the secret that we were.
I have found valleys more felicitous,
hidden and full of peace and godlier,
where leaf and wing to lighter music stir
and where no lyric is anonymous.

                 (1956)

The Old Bee House

"There by the plum trees is the bee house,"
I told the new guest airily,
"Its roof sags and the clapboards rattle."
He turned and stared at me.

"Inside the door are the hat with netting
and bellows to bring the young swarm home,
and just beyond are the large extractor
and the squares for the honeycomb."

"This is my house when the heart is injured,"
I said. "The wild sweet smell
of buckwheat honey or clover honey
can make it well."

I showed him the hives beyond the orchard;
slumped in the grass, they were squat and gray.
He tipped his hat with a frightened gesture
and rushed away.

And when he went, the bee house vanished
and the hives were gone and the trees were dead;
and the years that a dream of childhood smothered
were back on my head.

Ice Storm

The language of the heart would desecrate
the chastity of this moon-blinded night,
these iridescent trees of ice, these great
ascetic areas of silver light

that have been fields before the winter rain
froze on the snow to magnify the moon.
The trees and vines tinkle a thin refrain
like a glass windbell's tune.

Let those who go abroad be solitary,
stifle the heart and see how this unknown
and brittle world, unreal and legendary,
was filmed in crystal for the mind alone.

(1940; 1946)

Leafage of Snow

How would the green lush growth encounter frost?
With odor and decay.
There rejoice that leaf and blade are lost
before death's hands are on the season crossed.
Nature is much more easily embossed
with all but the simplicities away.

And we, as well, invite the matchless fair
when we are stripped and shriven.
When all that grows of earth lies gaunt and bare
then is the hour auspicious to prepare
for the white foliage of upper air,
the snow that falls from heaven.

(1941; 1946)

A Meadow Moreover

A sound like that of a meadowlark
poured heaven through the city park,
and though it died false, my memory
had crept through the notes and fluttered free.
It was off and away where a meadow stands
out in the clean undeeded lands,
past time, past even a need of name,
a place where only the children came.
The bobolinks sang where a tall grass sway
made a green salaam, and the flowers ran gay
through a moving quilt; wild strawberries bled
till the thought like the taste was comforted.
And the moss was soft—of a finer class
than the soft of the friendly ticklegrass.
That free is a child's word none deny—
this, heaven and earth both testify,
that God is a meadow in some high way,
a meadow moreover revealed in ours
where only the children find the flowers.

(1955)

Loveliest Blossom

When you are eager in the tiny portion
that is your garden, when you are tying strings
to give the stalks of the sweet peas their balance
so flowers may alight on them like wings
of pastel butterflies; when you appraise
with glowing face the lilies and carnations
(scent is to charm and color to amaze),
I think: she has not found the loveliest blossom.
There is a flower full of mystery
between this wall and that, amid this green.
I found it but to bear it back to secret.
It is a flower God and I have seen,
and I not till I looked at it with Him.
Hidden and unpredictable and shy,
it was not given to be shared, not even with you,
little lover of fragrance.
(Oh, with you least of all!)
Plucked from the soft soil of your unawareness,
uprooted from my silence, it would die.
I keep it then, God's individual favor,
the private bloom I scent my storerooms by.

(1954)

The Cedar Tree

In the beginning, in the unbeginning
of endlessness and of eternity,
God saw this tree.
He saw these cedar branches bending low
under the full exhaustion of the snow.
And since He set no wind of day to rising,
this burden of beauty and this burden of cold,
(whether the wood breaks or the branches hold)
must be of His devising.

There is a cedar similarly decked
deep in the winter of my intellect
under the snow, the snow,
the scales of light its limitations tell.

I clasp this thought: from all eternity
God who is good looked down upon this tree
white in the weighted air,
and of another cedar reckoned well.
He knew how much each tree, each twig could bear.
He counted every snowflake as it fell.

(1945; 1984)

Deer in the Open

Deer had been sighted near, the neighbors said,
so we were watching when we saw them go
lightly through fields where hazel brush had spread.
We had the clearest picture of the doe

leaping along. A shaft of sunlight caught her
like some excited hunter shouting "Here!"
We saw at once how open land and water
no less than cages desecrate the deer.

The scattered trees gave scant screen to a stranger
that field and pasture marked for rudest show,
and traffic had its wolf ways to endanger
the lovely indecision of the doe.

This then is why I sent word to the grieving
Spirit that keeps the woods, why I set down
the whereabouts and chances for retrieving
these tawny jewels lost to a forest crown.

In the Dells

I have never seen trees so slim and tall
as these in the canyon; I have never seen
such proud trees, so arrogant, so serene.
I have never heard a singing bird call
with such clear dignity as this flying crow
over the water sawing the air with sound.
Sunlight puts king's feet on this royal ground
feeling its pleasure where the soft ferns grow.
I think if I stood long enough in this green
cool place that never again would I dare to be
bowed by even a faint humility.
I think I would hold my head like a young queen.

The Late of Leaf

Tempted am I to tell the locust
what every pale green willow knows—
that spring is here. Her mind is focused
on sleeping and remembered snows.

She is like those who, though the ringing
of alleluia be heard,
still miss the resurrection, clinging
still to the bleak disproven word.

Birds and Lessons for Life

Bird at Daybreak

Here is a small bird cast as John the Baptist
who from my treetops is inspired to say:
I come from heaven to prepare the way.
Now in the east approach the feet of day.

Day will reward you well, my little bird,
who make his coming such enchanting news,
who with the sweetest music I have heard
unloose the golden lachet of his shoes.

(1938)

Bird at Evening

Here is a very Magdalen of bird
weeping her music at the feet of day,
who in a moment more will be interred
and in his shroud of silver laid away.

This is the bird that lately had anointed
the radiant flesh with the cool oil of song.
These feet are still; the night is three days long.

Henceforth the story of this bird will live
enclosed forever in day's narrative.
This shall be told of her
wherever any poet is appointed
as day's biographer.

(1939)

181

Out of the Storm

The lemon air hung paralyzed
and not a leaf stirred in the lanes,
when sky, like spirit, was surprised
by sudden lightning veins.

Clouds gave a blue bold threat of wind
frenzied with freedom; overhead,
where the great dome of day inclined,
a slow black terror spread.

And then the wind came pouring through.
A bird flew up exultantly
out of my breast, it seemed. I knew
its emptied nest in me.

I had not thought such joy could be
hidden in me and take to air.
My dark now sings with mystery.
What other bird is there?

Nighthawks Flying

At dusk the nighthawks dip and fly
between the purple bluffs and me;
black wings against a tinted sky—
they make a strange uncertainty

of sane things that the daylight said,
as if a word I chanced to miss;
a prelude I had never read
were needed to interpret this.

(1926)

Like Kildeers Crying

Tonight I lost my heart's whole sense of you—
I could not find you any way I turned.
Even your swift impetuous words that burned
into my mind were cold and palely blue

with the small death that any frail words meet
within a moment too profound for them.
The dusk was velvet, bending on a stem
like a crushed flower soft and April-sweet.

When suddenly, out where half-lights edge grey air,
a kildeer lifted from a glassy pond,
seeking the shadows of the field beyond,
flying and crying with a wild despair.

I lost you then. My thoughts like kildeers flew
over a bright pond where day was dying;
the dusk held nothing save their lonely crying,
and nothing mattered—neither love nor you.

(1928; 1939)

Poet of a Gentler Time

On a shrill street he mourns his nightingales
through whom love spoke; he writes in weightless verse
his anguish at the absence of the lark.
I come to him; I bring him rueful tales
that the small birds of indigence rehearse
on the bare branches of a city park.

Surely, he cries, where towers make wilderness,
and stones supplant the moss, and song gives way
to raucous speech, you must in tears confess
a most unmusical and loveless day.

My words torment him with the prick of arrows.
Not soon, not ever will he understand
that love may learn the accent of the sparrows,
having no larks or nightingales at hand.

(1940; 1946)

For a Silent Poet

Song was a wild bird and it came unbidden.
It settled down across the darkened air
to a gray branch in a dull orchard hidden.
One morning it was there.

Feathers of luster and a polished beak,
you cried in your delight, what is this bird
that in one space of music seems to speak
the note and the note's word?

It came from meadows seasonless and boundless
into your orchard for a summer stay,
and then one night you saw it lift on soundless
white wings and float away.

Weep not that visit of a brief duration.
You are a guest yourself and you must know
that in you lie the instincts of migration,
and where the bird went, one day you will go.

(1940; 1946)

Robin at Dusk

I can go starved the whole day long,
draining a stone, eating a husk,
and never hunger till a song
breaks from a robin's throat at dusk.

I am reminded only then
how far from day and human speech,
how far from the loud world of men
lies the bright dream I strain to reach.

Oh, that a song of mine could burn
the air with beauty so intense,
sung with a robin's unconcern
for any mortal audience!

Perhaps I shall learn presently
his secret when the shadows stir,
and I shall make one song and be
aware of but one Listener.

(1927; 1939)

Birds

That God made birds is surely in His favor.
I write them as His courtesies of love.
Hidden in leaves, they offer me sweet savor
of lightsome music; when they streak above

my garden wall they brush my scene with color.
They are embroideries upon the grass.
I write the gayest stitched-in blossoms duller
than birds which change their patterns as I pass.

I nurse a holy envy of St. Francis
who lured the birds to nestle at his breast.
Yet I am grateful for this one which dances
across my lawn, a reckless anapest.

Subjects for gratitude push up my living
praise to a sum that tempts the infinite;
but birds deserve one whole psalm of thanksgiving
and these words are my antiphon for it.

(1956)

Fair Lines Forgotten

Rare was the bird that slipped my grasp.
I saw it on a mental bough
and leaped before I guessed its fright
at movement in diminished light.
I rue my hurry now.

If it had perished in the south
or found a nest in other lands,
'twould grieve me less than this escape.
Full robbed am I who stand agape
with feathers in both hands.

The Hermit Thrush

Not once have I stood motionless and breathless
on greenest lanes and heard a song rise clear.
I never feasted on that forest music
which one small bird intended me to hear.

That bird was mine by a most sacred kinship
yet met we not in time and traffic rush.
Hence I have only documents of longing
to prove me sister to the hermit thrush.

Yet past all loss, heaven leans down to argue:
ah, in love's denser wood and far more fair
sings the more hidden soul its purer music.
Enter, it says, oh, go and listen there.

Doxology

God fills my being to the brim
with floods of His immensity.
I drown within a drop of Him
whose sea-bed is infinity.

The Father's will is everywhere
for chart and chance His precept keep.
There are no beaches to His care
nor cliffs to pluck from His deep.

The Son is never far away from me
for presence is what love compels.
Divinely and incarnately
He draws me where His mercy dwells.

And lo, myself am the abode
of Love, the third of the Triune,
the primal surge and sweep of God
and my eternal claimant soon!

Praise to the Father and the Son
and to the Spirit! May I be,
O Water, Wave and Tide in One,
Thine animate doxology.

(1946; 1984)

Jessica Powers —Chronology
(Agnes Jessika Powers)

Grandparents' families from County Waterford, Ireland;
       immigrated to Mauston, Wisconsin; Scottish-Irish
       background

Siblings: Catherine Dorothy (1899-1916) called Dorothy
       John Trainer (1901-1977)
       James Daniel (1906-1956) called Daniel

1905   February 7: born in Mauston, Wisconsin, to John Powers
       (1865-1918) and Delia Trainer Powers (1867-1925)

       February 26: baptized at St. Patrick's Church, Mauston
       Godparents: John Walsh / Nellie Keegan
       Priest: Rev. Peter Becker

1911-1916   Educated in rural school

1916   Dorothy dies of tuberculosis

1916   Jessica attends "the Sisters' school in Mauston"; is
       encouraged to write by Dominican Sister Lucille
       Massart

1918-1922   Attends local high school in Mauston

1918   Solemn Communion

1918   May 22: John Powers dies of heart attack

1919   Confirmation (Jessica Lucille Powers)

* * *

1922-1923   Attends Marquette University in Milwaukee;
       enrolls in school of journalism since liberal arts school
       does not accept women

1923-1924	Does secretarial work in Chicago; spends free time reading poetry in libraries
1925	September 12: Delia Trainer Powers dies
1925-1936	Lives on the farm; two brothers eventually marry; some poems published in local papers; contributes to a column entitled "The Percolator," in *The Milwaukee Sentinel*
1936	Spends a few months in Chicago
1937-1941	Moves to New York: lives with Jessie and Anton Pegis; becomes member of Catholic Poetry Society of America; in 1939 first book of poetry, *The Lantern Burns*, is published by Clifford Laube, suburban editor of *The New York Times* and associate editor of *Spirit*

* * *

1941	Enters Carmel of the Mother of God in Milwaukee, Wisconsin
1942	April 25: clothing day—takes the name Sister Miriam of the Holy Spirit
1943	May 8: first profession of vows
1946	May 8: perpetual profession
1946	Cosmopolitan Science and Art Service, New York publishes her second book of poetry *The Place of Splendor*—Dr. Anton Pegis helpful in this project
1955	Elected prioress; *The Little Alphabet* published
1958	Carmelites move to new Carmel in Pewaukee, Wisconsin

* * *

1958-1961	Second term as prioress
1959-1960	October to October in tuberculosis sanatorium
1964-1967	Another term as prioress
1972	Reno Carmel's artistic printing of *The Mountain Sparrow*
1980	Christmas booklet "Journey to Bethlehem" printed
1981	Italian translation of *The Place of Splendor*
1984	*The House at Rest* published privately
1988	July 9-10: approved manuscript of selected poetry assembled by Sr. Regina Siegfried, ASC and Bp. Robert Morneau
	August 17: suffers severe stroke
	August 18: dies
	August 22: funeral liturgy at Carmel of the Mother of God, Pewaukee, Wisconsin; burial at Holy Cross Cemetery, Milwaukee, Wisconsin

Books published by Jessica Powers

The Lantern Burns. New York: The Monastine Press, 1939.

The Place of Splendor. New York: Cosmopolitan Science and Art Service, Inc., 1946.

The Little Alphabet. 1955.

Mountain Sparrow. (10 poems by Jessica Powers) published by the Carmel of Reno, 1972

Journey to Bethlehem. Christmas poems, privately published, 1980.

The House at Rest. Privately published, 1984.

Bibliography of Secondary Sources

Reviews of *The Lantern Burns*

Barret, Alfred, in *Thought,* 15, No. 58 (Sept., 1940), 530-531.

Binsse, Harry, in *Commonweal,* 32, No. 5 (May, 1940), 107.

Feeney, Leonard, in *America,* 63, No. 7 (May 25, 1940), 192.

Kolars, Mary, in *Spirit,* 6, No. 5 (November, 1939), 152-153.

Reilly, Joseph, in *The Catholic World,* 151 (May, 1940), 252.

Sign, 19, No. 5 (December, 1939), 312-313.

Reviews of *The Place of Splendor*

Brunini, John G., in *Spirit,* 14, No. 2 (May, 1947), 57-59.

Hughes, Josephine N., in *America,* 77, No. 21 (August 23, 1947), 584.

Laube, Clifford J., in *Thought,* 22 (June, 1947), 246-248.

Commonweal, 46 (July 25, 1947), 361.

Sign, 26, No. 12 (July, 1947), 57.

Reviews of *The House at Rest*

Howell, Olga M., in *St. Anthony Messenger* (June, 1987).

Morneau, Robert F., in *Emmanuel* 91, No. 10 (December, 1985), 591-592.

Articles

Baldwin, S. M. Luke, SSND. "Burns the Great Lantern." Catholic *World,* 168 (February, 1949), 354-361.

Berlingeri, Francesca. "Una Nuova Voce Poetica Del Carmelo: Jessica Powers." *Humanitas* (Brescia), 13, No. 7 (luglio, 1958), 536-542.

Geigel, Winifred F. (S. M. Teresa de la Cruz, CSJ). "A Comparative Study of the Poetry of Jessica Powers and St. John of the Cross." Unpublished thesis, St. John University, 1960.

Hopkins, J. G. E. "A Modern Poet with a Medieval Ideal." *America,* 61, No. 21 (September 2, 1939), 498-499. [Two paragraphs on Jessica Powers].

McDonnell, Thomas P. "The Nun as Poet." *Spirit,* 26, No. 1 (March, 1959), 20-26.

Morneau, Robert F. "Come is the Love Song." *Emmanuel,* 91, No. 10 (December, 1985), 546-551.

Morneau, Robert F. "The Garments of God." *Emmanuel,* 92, No. 5 (June, 1986), 264-267/287.

Morneau, Robert F. "A Refugee God." *Emmanuel,* 92, No. 10 (December, 1986).

Morneau, Robert F. "An Experience of God: Reflections of a Poet's Journey." *Emmanuel,* 93, No. 9 (November, 1987), 486-493.

Schaeverling, Margaret. "Sister Miriam of the Holy Spirit." *Magnificat,* 83, No. 4 (February, 1949), 168-172.

Siegfried, Regina, ASC. "Jessica Powers: The Paradox of Light and Dark." *Studia Mystica,* 7, No.1 (Spring, 1984), 28-45.

Shufletavski, Dorothy. "Fosterling of Night." Clarke College *Labarum.* Dubuque, Iowa, 1945, 252.

Timothy, Sister Mary. "The Silent Poet." *Spirit,* 27, No. 2 (May, 1960), 52-57.